M[illegible] Fish Bowl

A Memoir of a Pastor's Daughter and a Pastor's Wife

By B. Joan Taylor

B. Joan Taylor

My Life in a Fish Bowl

Cover Design: Ryan Rawn
Layout: Cam Taylor

Published in Canada by Infocus Publishing
ISBN 978-0-9950968-0-6

Dedication

This book is dedicated to my husband, Keith, who has loved and supported me for over 60 years. Also to our children - Beth, Cam, and Marilou who have always been our pride and joy. A special thanks to Cam for his invaluable assistance in bringing this project to completion.

Preface

This is my story with events as I remember them. I realize that my siblings may have different memories from mine. Even our children may not recall events in the same way I did.

I was born in a church. Furthermore, I spent all my growing-up years in a house provided by the church (a parsonage) as a PK (preacher's kid). I married a pastor so spent many of my adult years in parsonages as a PW (pastor's wife). So I feel like I have lived my life in a fishbowl. As a PK, I was often reminded by my mother that I was expected to be an example. As a PW, I felt that how I lived my life, how well I took care of the parsonage, and how we raised our children were all under scrutiny.

I never aspired to being a pastor's wife. In fact, I often said that I would *never* marry a pastor! I had watched my dad being criticized and my mother feeling the burden of other people's problems weighing on her. When I read a book called, "How to Be a Pastor's Wife and Like It," I scoffed at the idea. But looking back, I realize that God was preparing me for a life of service and I am thankful for all the lessons he has taught me over the years. It wasn't always easy, but I learned to love the people we were ministering to and the joy of knowing that I had a small part in their spiritual growth.

Having turned 80, I feel that it is time to get my story into print. Life is good. I have become a much more confident person, having lived a life of purpose and meaning.

I feel that I am just an ordinary person who serves an extraordinary God.

Chapter 1:

Humble Beginnings

My family when I was a baby

My story began in the month of February of 1935, in the midst of the Great Depression. Times were tough and the winters were severe, temperatures plummeting to 60 below zero. My parents were poor and my birth was particularly difficult. When the time came that my mother's pain became unbearable, Dad realized the urgency of the situation and went for the doctor. The birth would not take place in a hospital where there would be an attending physician or nurses. My parents had no money for that. It was out of the kindness of his heart that Dr. Stirrit ventured up the back stairs of a small apartment above the church, to assist the poor preacher's wife with what turned out to be a breech birth. Many times my mother reminded me of the pain which she described as "the worst pain on earth." I can only imagine how excruciating the experience was as I had to be turned without the aid of an anesthetic. But my dad, Murdo Campbell, recorded in his book *Poor Yet Possessing* how he felt about my entry into the world: "On the 16th day of February, our second daughter, Barbara Joan, was born. She was a little round, plump bundle of delight to the household..."

My parents were meant for each other. I always loved to hear their love story which Dad told and re-told in his sermons. He left Holland, Manitoba where he had been raised on a farm to pursue work in the harvest fields of Saskatchewan. His search ended at a place called Webb where he met a man who owned a farm in southern Saskatchewan. Dad was broke and when the man offered him a job he gladly accepted. His destination was a farm seventeen miles from the nearest town where my mother was cooking for the threshing crew that wheat farmers acquired each fall. With her sister, Ada, Mom was making breakfast when Murdo, the newest hired hand, came around the corner one fateful harvest morning. When Ada spied him, she turned to my mother and said, "Here comes a man that you'll be cooking for for the rest of your life!" Her words turned out to be prophetic because Mom and Dad fell in love and were subsequently married. That marriage, which took place May 3, 1930, lasted for 63+ years. But I've heard Dad remind us many times that *he* was the one who made the breakfast! He was a good cook and made the best biscuits.

My parents on their wedding day, May 3, 1930

Mom and Dad didn't have an easy life. They experienced many reverses in business ventures and often didn't know where to go next in their endeavours to make a living. Mother, unlike her husband, had been raised in a Christian home but when she met Dad, she temporarily forgot about her commitment to the Lord. Dad was always so much fun and Mom joined him in his pursuit of happiness in the early years of their marriage. Their first child, Roderick McLeod, was born in 1931, followed seventeen months later by Eveline Alice in 1933. That was the year that their lives turned around when at the Admiral Camp meeting on a hot July day, my dad heard God's call and had a conversion experience that completely changed his destiny. Soon after, he was called to preach and 1935 found him in his first church in Swift Current, Saskatchewan, the one in which I was born.

Pastoring in those depression years was challenging, to say the least. Churches in the Holiness Movement Church that we were affiliated with were small and parsonages inadequate for growing families. Money was scarce but God always provided for the family. Sometimes our needs were met when Dad reluctantly applied for "relief." I remember Dad talking about the Christmas of 1934 when he and Mom had twenty-five cents to spend for the family's gifts. But Dad, always a man of faith, was devoted to God and never looked back once his calling was clear.

Chapter 2:

My Nomadic Life Begins

Mom, Dad, Rod, Eveline, myself and Shirley in 1941

When I was about six months old, my dad was appointed to Wildwood, Alberta where in August, 1937, my sister, Shirley Ann was born. Life was a series of adjustments for our family as three years was the limit for a pastor to stay at one church in those early years. That summer saw us on the move again, this time to D'Arcy, Saskatchewan. While Mom was recuperating from our move and the birth of her fourth child, I was sent to stay with a church farm family for several weeks. By this time the oldest, Rod, had just turned six and Eveline was four. Although I was only two and a half, I have memories of that experience. I enjoyed all the attention I got from the family who had a teenage son. There were many new experiences on the farm, one being eggnog, a delicious new treat. My most poignant memory is of myself lying face down on a Toronto couch (I'm not sure how it got that name!) feeling lonesome for my family but not wanting to tell anyone. Another of my very early memories was of my imaginary friend I called Barley.

When my mom asked me to help with the dishes I would say, "Let Barley do it!" Sometimes it worked and sometimes it didn't.

Because Dad hadn't had any Bible school training, (although he had only a Grade eight education, he was an intelligent man and a lover of books) his next move was to McCord, Saskatchewan where he pursued biblical studies while pastoring the church. I have some vivid memories of the time we spent in McCord. The parsonage was located in the country, across from the local cemetery. About half a mile from our place (distances, for me, are best remembered in miles) was the Willie Belsher farm. They had seventeen children (not all of them still at home) with kids the ages of all of us – and more! We liked to meet at the creek where we went swimming. One sad experience for me was the day that I took my doll into the water with me. Dolls were not waterproof in those days and after the swim, all her "skin" peeled off!

When I was about five a very frightening experience took place when my three-year-old sister, Shirley's nose started to bleed profusely and it just wouldn't stop. In my mind's eye I can see what looked like a tub full of blood and I was really scared, thinking she was going to die. Swift Current was the nearest hospital and we were many miles from there. But it soon became urgent that she get there as quickly as possible. We didn't have very reliable cars in those days so a friend from the church drove my parents to the hospital. They gave her transfusions and, thankfully, she lived! Another memory of those two years was us kids all contracting the red measles. We were kept inside with all the blinds closed for what seemed like a long time.

We spent many happy days playing at the haystack which was located between our home and the Belshers. We had a special call we made whenever we wanted to meet them there. I will never forget one Sunday when, against our parents' instructions, we snuck off to meet our friends. Rod was nine, Eveline seven, I was five and Shirley was three. When we arrived home, Mom was waiting for us with her trusty fly swatter! I was quite indignant because Shirley was too young to be punished and I thought I should have been considered faultless too because, I argued, I wouldn't have gone without my older siblings' leading the way. That was the first time I understood the price that had to be paid for disobedience. As I recall, a fly swatter on the hand really stings! It was the only punishment inflicted on me by my mother. I have one memory of my dad patting me on the bottom as I was stomping up the stairs. I don't even remember what misdemeanor I was guilty of but I'm quite sure I deserved the discipline, which deeply wounded my dignity.

The church in McCord was vibrant -- a good place to be. Dad enjoyed the congregation of upbeat and fairly prosperous people, as well as the stimulation of having the Bible school students in attendance in the winter. One memory of that, which is more a memory because of it being retold, involved my night spent with the Bible school students. During an evening service when I fell asleep, someone carried me to the basement, where the male students had their sleeping quarters, and left me on one of the student's beds. After the service, the family journeyed home without me. When they realized that Joanie was not in the car, a phone call assured them that I was safe with the Bible school students (having been moved to the girls' sleeping quarters) and my parents could recover me in the morning. It was a wintry evening and no one considered it necessary to make the trip back that night. After all, it was a mile away!

Chapter 3:

Life in Cadillac

Our next move was to Cadillac, about 40 miles west of McCord. It was not one of the choicest places to live. The countryside was barren with few trees. The community was predominantly French and there was a very large Roman Catholic Church across from our house, which was on the main street of the town. I recall a visit to that building when the priest took us through and explained all the religious symbolism of their faith. I was awestruck by the beauty of the place and wondered why our churches, in contrast, were so bare and unattractive. At the conclusion of our tour, we were treated to ice cream, which was served to us in the rectory by the priest's housekeeper.

Our plain little frame church, located next door to the parsonage on the corner was beside the town hall. One year the circus came to town, taking place in that hall. The only problem was we weren't allowed to go. Our dad, for some reason, felt that the circus was not a good thing for his family to attend. It was hard to be the only kids in town who couldn't be part of such an amazing event. After the Saturday night dances that were held in the hall, we collected dozens of beer bottles that earned us a little spending money (a penny a bottle, as I recall). One Saturday night in his drunken stupor, a man staggered into our house and in the morning Dad found him asleep at the bottom of the stairs! No one even considered locking the doors at night or when you went uptown. Such was life in that small village.

There was a convent at Ponteix, about ten miles away, where my sister, Eveline, took piano lessons from the sisters. That was another building of which I stood in awe because of its beauty. Cadillac was the place where my piano lessons began when I was in Grade one. One of the ladies from the church, Vi Campbell (no relation), was my teacher. We had to walk to her family's farm which was about three long miles from town. Those memories are not among my most precious. The final memorable event that took place in Cadillac was at our farewell when a farm dog took a big chunk out of the leg of one of the boys. That quickly ended our frivolity.

My memories of Cadillac are kind of a blur since we were there twice for a year each time. The first time I was in Grade one and the next time in Grade five. I absolutely loved my grade one teacher and from that day on decided I wanted to teach. There were four grades in each room and, the second time around, I was in the same room with Eveline and Rod, who were both in Grade eight. Eveline had started school at five and Rod at six so they were a grade apart. But in Grade three, Rod had a teacher who didn't seem to appreciate his superior abilities and kept him from passing his grade. In Cadillac, our teacher, who attended our church, was frustrated with the behaviour of some of her pupils, including the church kids. One day she informed us that she was *Miss Campbell* (no relation, but a sister of my piano teacher) whether she was in church, in school or on the street! It wasn't hard to see to whom she was speaking. One day she sent Rod to the blackboard to write a letter. For the inside address he wrote, "Cadillac Jail." For some reason, Miss Campbell did not appreciate the humour!

A few other memories are vivid ones. At the back of our property was a small barn-like building with a loft (probably used to accommodate the animals during horse and buggy days). We turned the upstairs into a concert hall and presented a variety show for the neighbours. We had skits and songs, some of the kids danced and everyone was charged ten cents admission. This, of course, was the brainchild of my brother, Rod, who was an entrepreneur before the word was invented. The money, people were told, was to go to the Red Cross. The war was on at the time so this was quite a credible idea. However, when Dad heard of our scheme, he made us return the money to the people who came to the show. It had seemed like such a good idea! Rod, always the leader, had his followers and he liked to impress people. His desire to be the "big shot" led him to take money from the cocoa can where our tithe was kept, purchase a stash of gum and fill his pockets with it (doublemint gum, he recalls). He was passing it out at school and, of course, made quite an impact. Dad, however, was not impressed. Rod got lots of spankings those days and I can remember being in an upstairs bedroom crying while he was being disciplined for his rebellious actions.

Dad was a strong believer in the admonitions of the book of Proverbs. In 23:13 it says: "Do not withhold discipline from a child; if you punish him with the rod, he will not die." Another verse (13:24) says: "He who spares the rod hates his son, but he who loves him is careful to discipline him." Dad loved his sons, Rod and later Ross, but sometimes I feel like the discipline meted out to them was too severe and didn't have the desired results. I am thankful that, in spite of the harsh discipline, my brothers still loved and respected my dad

One of the memories of Cadillac was the Saturday night baths. They took place in the kitchen in a round tin tub which was set up on a backless chair. We all took turns bathing, from the youngest to the oldest. Mom would add warm water after each bath so that by the time it was Dad's turn, there was a fair amount of not-so-clean water in the tub. One of those Saturday evenings there was a disaster when the entire contents of the tub landed upside down on the floor! What a mess! We always used an outdoor toilet (usually a two-seater) except in the wintertime. I felt sorry for Dad when he had to carry downstairs the contents of the inside toilet. Those were the days!

I remember lots of games of hopscotch during that time. How well I recall the night I was playing hopscotch with a boy I liked.

We could hardly see but that made it more fun! One of my special friends in Cadillac, Cynthia Buckwold, was Jewish. Her father, a shrewd man, owned the general store. I thought it strange that at Christmas time when we received our gifts, the Buckwold kids also received presents, much more elaborate than ours, from their parents. One year they got the most beautiful dolls, the envy of the girls in the town. And they didn't even believe in Jesus! Mr. Buckwold treated our family well. He always gave his loyal customers candy with their orders. Sugar rationing during the war made candy a very special treat. And He always had nylon stockings – for certain people. I can recall Paula, Cynthia's older sister, correcting her dad when he said they had no stockings. She knew better. Another event that stands out vividly in my memory was the spectacular fire that burned down several buildings, including the store and the Royal Bank. My friend's dad was the bank manager and the family lived in the apartment above the bank. It was a sad day for many and a tremendous loss to the small town.

Another achievement during my second year in Cadillac was learning to ride a bike. We only had a boy's bike so learning to ride, for me, was a huge challenge. Because I couldn't reach the pedals when I sat on the seat, I had to put my leg in between the frame, a very awkward position. There were many scraped knees and elbows during the process. At one point I remember not being able to get stopped, which resulted in my running into a parked vehicle.

A not-so-happy memory, which is embarrassing in retrospect, was the day that my little brother, Ross got his pinky finger caught in the screen door, cutting it nearly off. I was so frightened that I ran away, leaving someone else to look after him. I don't even remember who came to his rescue.

Chapter 4:

Killarney - My Happiest Childhood Years

After one year in Cadillac the first time, our next move was to Killarney, Manitoba, a lovely prairie town with lots of trees in the surrounding area and a beautiful lake nearby. It was a larger place than the villages we had lived in previously. I spent my happiest childhood years in that community with lots of memories of the good times. I had many friends there and loved school where I was a good student. I know that because of a report card in which the teacher had written, "Joan is an excellent student and it is a pleasure working with her." The report card is long gone but the words still stick in my memory. The kids in the neighbourhood had great fun playing games together when the weather was fit. After supper, we all met at the street light at the end of our block. *Run Sheep Run, Kick the Can,* and *Anti-I-Over* were among our favourite games. In the winter a nearby "mountain" provided countless hours of entertainment, especially the Christmas that our family gift was a toboggan, a source of great joy. In the summer we enjoyed swimming, and boating, whenever we had an opportunity, at Killarney Lake. There were no swimming lessons those days so I never did learn to swim but my sister, Eveline, swam like a fish. It seemed to come naturally to her. The annual fair was another highlight of our summer. I always entered my printing and writing in the fair and received prizes every year. My favourite ride was the Ferris wheel which seemed very high and scary in those days. How much smaller it has shrunk over the years! One significant event for me was when I was in Grade three when my teacher allowed my friends and me to present a play I had written. We had wonderful times playing school (I was always the teacher), playing house where we dressed up as bride and groom and held wedding ceremonies with curtains for our veils, going to birthday parties, and visiting my friend, Doris Baskerville's family farm where we happily played in the hayloft of their giant barn. The year that caused me much pain was the year that I contracted the mumps just before Easter holidays and couldn't go to the farm as planned. Another memory, which upset me because of its unfairness, was the day that a boy and I were carrying on a conversation when the teacher grabbed him, ripping his shirt while taking him into the hall to give him the strap (still an acceptable means of punishment at that time). I knew I was just as guilty as he.

Our family in Killarney, Rod wearing his cadet uniform

One memory that stands out above the others was the day that we were playing in my friend, Loreen Caswell's barn. There was a loft with a ladder that went up the side. We were taking turns getting into a gunny sack and allowing it to be lowered from an opening in the loft. When my turn came I was much braver than the others and let myself be put right into the sack, not reaching out to hold onto the ladder on the way down. Unfortunately, the rope which was tied around the corners of the bag, slipped off and I was lowered to the cement floor with a thud. The kids were terrified, thinking I might be dead. My hip bothered me for a while but otherwise I was okay. I can still recall my friend's mother's warning me that sometimes injuries like that will turn into cancer later. While still recovering from the fall, I can well remember how much it hurt as all of us school kids marched in a parade to the fairgrounds, burning Hitler in effigy to celebrate the end of the war. That was a moment to remember!

The war years provided me with other vivid memories as two of my uncles had answered the call for service. Uncle Bert Prosser (mom's brother) left from Killarney, after he had been training in Shiloh, Manitoba. That was a sad day for his wife who, with their two young children, lived with us for a while. Fortunately he came home after the war and they had four more children. My Uncle Lewis Radford (mom's half-brother), became a paratrooper. My grandmother was terrified that he would be in grave danger and might never return. But he did. Now 91, he still lives on the family farm. Another uncle, a brother of my dad's, was also in the service but his was a relatively safe posting - guarding the abdicated King Edward and his divorced wife, Wallace Simpson, in the Bahamas. He had also served in the First World War, lying about his age in order to enlist.

One of the happiest events of 1944 was the arrival of our little brother, Ross Alexander who brought a lot of fun into our lives. I well remember the day when Mom and Dad gave me the news that we were having a baby. After I was told not to tell (I really don't know why it was such a secret) I left for school and, meeting my friend, immediately shared the good news! Because he was 7-1/2

Our family is complete with the addition of baby Ross

years younger than Shirley, our youngest sibling, he received lots of attention. I remember trying to coax him to walk but he was 14 months old before he ventured out on his own. It bothered us kids when other children his age walked before he did. Though a very shy child, who clung closely to my mother's side, he later climbed out of his shell and became the "life of the party" in our family.

Another exciting family event that occurred that year was the accumulation of a beautiful 1938 maroon Chevrolet which an elderly friend loaned Dad to bring Mom and the new baby home from Brandon. When Dad returned the car, the man offered to sell it for the price of $549 (a price much lower than he could have gotten for it at that time). What a proud moment for our family! We had never owned such a beautiful vehicle.

Chapter 5:

Sibling Rivalry

My best friend during my childhood was my sister, Shirley. She was more compliant by nature than either Eveline or I, so we played together happily by the hour. Our favourite pastime was cut-out dolls. We cut pictures of furniture out of the catalogue to create a well-decorated home in which our dolls lived. We didn't have a lot of money for toys but we could afford new books of paper dolls periodically. Eveline was always very much my "big" sister because she assumed more responsibility around the house and seemed much older than the two years that separated us. She was very mature and at 13 went to work for a farm family some distance away. I can remember her telling us about that trip on the bus. Someone thought she was much older and offered her a cigarette! She was very efficient in many ways - very good at cleaning house (which I didn't enjoy - and still don't!) and very fast at everything. I thought she was the best piano player in the world! She could play anything by ear (a gift I did not possess). I remember feeling so proud of her when she played the hit parade songs during recess and noon breaks at school when the kids gathered around the piano. Dad would take her to meetings to be his pianist. It was no

Shirley and I enjoying a warm summer day

secret that he had a very special love for Eveline. Everyone said she looked like him, even from the moment she made her entrance into the world.

I always thought that Mom loved Eveline more than she did me. I struggled many years with what has been called the Middle Child Syndrome. I was not only the middle of three girls but also the middle of five with a brother and sister older and a brother and sister younger. Because Eveline was so talented musically and such a good worker, I felt I could never measure up. And Shirley was the pretty one. She was born with beautiful blond curly hair and she had the face of an angel. Everybody remarked that Shirley was such a doll but never once did anyone say anything like that to me! She was also a wonderful musician and my mother would often refer to Shirley's lovely touch on the piano. I was a hopeless piano pupil and finally was allowed to quit lessons when I was about 14 and had completed Grade 6 (sort of). My mother thought the money would be better spent on voice lessons which became part of my experience a couple of years later.

My relationship with my older brother, Rod, was one of hero-worship. He was a very confident person who made friends easily and was always the centre of attention. He would listen to the hockey games on Saturday night and I would sit beside him, not having much interest in the game but wanting to be with him. I would cheer when Foster Hewitt enthusiastically proclaimed, "He shoots, he scores!" Another thing I would do with Rod was play Monopoly. That was one of our Christmas presents in Killarney and we kids spent countless hours playing the game (and arguing!). I would even go into Rod's room at night and play with him, just the two of us. We three sisters shared a bedroom while he had one of his own across the hall.

At the Admiral Camp one year, Rod, ever the ringleader, had bought some cigarettes and wanted all of us to smoke them so no one would tell. However, I had signed a WCTU (Women's Christian Temperance Union) pledge when I was nine in which I vowed that I would never touch alcohol or tobacco. I was very loyal to that vow and refused to smoke. Neither have I ever taken a drink. But I was also loyal to my brother and no matter what he did I never squealed on him.

Because our three-year time limit for pastors was up, far too soon we had to move. It was a sad day for everyone, including my dad. Our church in Killarney was small but Dad looked beyond his own congregation and made it his mission to visit every home in town and, if they agreed, have prayer with the people. He made a lasting impression on the residents. Furthermore, because of his heart for evangelism, he wasn't content to limit himself to one little church. Some of the time we went to a nearby town for a service and he also began a ministry in a little country school. It was not uncommon for us to attend Sunday School and church in the morning, rush off to another appointment in the afternoon and come back for a service in the evening.

My growing-up years were mobile years when I felt rootless. We never lived close to grandparents, aunts, uncles or cousins. I was always having to say goodbye to friends, vowing that I would never forget them. Some friendships lasted for a while but many did not survive. From birth to the completion of high school we had moved nine times. I attended school in Manitoba, Saskatchewan and Alberta. Our vacations were spent going from camp meeting to camp meeting. When we lived in Manitoba, we attended the Killarney Camp but Dad maintained a strong connection with the Admiral Camp in Saskatchewan where he had been converted in 1933 and we often attended there as well. During our stay in Edmonton, our camp was at Wildwood, Alberta. We had good times at those camps. One memory from the Wildwood Camp was of a Scottish lady, Jean Burns, who later became a missionary to Egypt. She used to sing to us girls at night when we didn't want to settle down to sleep. She had a beautiful voice and we loved the folk songs she entertained us with.

Because music was a priority in our home, we were all given piano lessons, whether we wanted to take them or not. I have my mother to thank that I can play the piano today because I hated practicing with a passion! My older brother was allowed to quit for the same reason and many times he has expressed regret that our parents did not make him persevere. Us girls always liked singing and in our teen years formed a trio that was pretty good, if I do say so myself! I remember the first solo I sang when I was only about eight, "No One Ever Cared for Me Like Jesus."

Another one of Dad's outreach ventures during our stay at Killarney was a radio broadcast over CKX in Brandon, Manitoba. I was eight or nine when we drove sixty miles on Tuesday morning to be on the air at 7:30 a.m. It was a family affair, Mom playing the piano (even on the day that Ross was born), the rest of us singing and Dad bringing a message. I will never forget the theme song, "Tis the Blessed Hour of Prayer." But how I hated rising at the unearthly hour of 5:00 a.m.! Going to bed early the night before was just as difficult. Those who know me best know I am NOT a morning person!

Chapter 6:

Memories of Our Year in Swift Current

When we were sent back to Cadillac for the second time, Dad became discontented in that little church which, he felt, was going nowhere. He made plans to build a home for the family in Swift Current so we would have a place to live while he pursued a ministry in evangelism. He was able to acquire a lot for $100 and, as I recall, an elevator annex for $500 which provided the lumber for the house. The bonds that we children had purchased during the war were cashed in to pay for the chimney in the new house. The basement was unfinished for the entire year that we lived there. The toilet was located at the far end of the basement (there was no bathroom) so you stumbled over piles of stones to reach it. But it certainly beat the outdoor biffies that we had had everywhere else! It was the only home our family lived in that was not provided by the church.

The house that Dad built for the family in Swift Current

On one unforgettable Sunday, the basement became my haven when I had sorely embarrassed my mother in front of the whole congregation (which was pretty small). Dad was away in some evangelistic endeavour and Mom had asked me to take 2-1/2-year old Rossie home in his stroller. I strongly objected and stomped off in a huff. However, the closer I got to home the worse I felt. I was convinced that I would get a good, well-deserved spanking when Mom got home. I stayed in the basement as long as I could and when I surfaced Mom just gave me a lecture about how disappointed she was in me. I felt like two cents! It hurt me as much as any spanking ever could.

Other than the Swift Current house, we lived in humble dwellings called parsonages where furniture was supplied by the church. Some of it was well-used furniture that members of the congregation had discarded. My mother, with the help of my handy-man dad, used her creativity to transform many an old house into an attractive home for her family. She saved and scrimped so she could buy carpets for the bare floors. These we got from the Brandon Woolen Mills where rags were transformed into rugs, with a nominal charge. She was in every sense a homemaker. She loved to cook and always served tasty meals. Her pies and buns were unequaled. She was a fastidious housekeeper and chased dirt mercilessly. She sewed hand-me-down clothes for us girls so that we were always well dressed, in spite of the lack of resources. Some of the materials came from Mom's rich relatives in Kingston, Ontario. Whenever boxes came, we all eagerly awaited the view of new items that emerged. Sometimes we were disappointed with the contents. Mom always made even our coats so the year that I got my first boughten coat was a thrill. As we got older, Mom took in boarders to help supplement our meagre income. She was thrifty and provided a balance for our generous father who was more of a free spender. He took me to buy a pair of shoes when I was about 14 and paid the scandalous price of $9.00 for them. During the years when there was no salary, we depended totally on people's generosity. In farming communities our income included chickens, eggs, beef or garden produce. There were times when all the money we got was in the offering and sometimes my absent-minded dad forgot to take it up!

A couple of very significant defining moments occurred during that year in Swift Current. I had two good friends, which made us a threesome - not a healthy arrangement when you are eleven years old. When two of us were together we talked about the missing member and I was sure it happened when I wasn't there. I will never forget the day that a girl in my grade six class met me at the bottom of the flight of stairs that led up to the entrance of Central School and confronted me with these words, "I hate you like poison." I was devastated. As I have become more mature, I realize that it was probably jealously because I know I was "the teacher's pet." That teacher, Miss Roney even sent me to the store to buy her cigarettes! When I told my friends about my devastating encounter with the girl whose name I have forgotten, they came up with a clever scheme, so they must have thought. I received in the mail an invitation to attend the birthday party of the girl who had said she hated me. I was elated, thinking she didn't hate me after all. I shared my delight with my friends, who began to feel quite uncomfortable. Before the day arrived, they had to confess that it was a practical joke and there was no party. I have never liked practical jokes since that day! To me there was nothing funny about it. Besides I always remembered Mom's account of receiving what she thought was a box of chocolates for Christmas one year, when inside there was a chunk of coal.

One event that was significant that year when I was in Grade six was a posture contest that the teacher initiated. We all marched around the classroom and she picked out the person with the best posture, then the next until the end. Always a person who walked with my head held high, I was second. The guy who was first (and looked like a wooden soldier) was also my competitor in academics as we took turns being first in the class. Some of the happy moments in school, that year and others were the spelling bees. I was almost always the last person standing. One year in about Grade four I spelled the world "aisle" incorrectly, making it "isle" instead. Disappointing!

One of the girls in our three-some, Pat Whalen, was my best friend and we spent much more time together. Her family was affluent. As an only child, she had many advantages – I admired her beautiful clothes and her cocker spaniel named Bonnie. Both her parents worked, not a common thing at that time. Often during that year I would tell my mother that I was going to Pat's house, then we'd head for downtown where we went to movies most Saturday afternoons. We saw some wonderful shows! I couldn't quite understand why they were prohibited by our church – they were so good -- dog and horse stories, all clean and wholesome. But I felt very guilty about my deception and would often think of the motto which hung in our home that read, "Go no place that you would not want to be found when Jesus comes; Say nothing you would not want to be saying when Jesus comes…" One of the big problems was that we got no allowance so I had to steal money to pay for the movies. There was always change in Dad's pockets or sitting around on shelves. One very scary thing happened one day. Mom had given me money to buy bread, I think it was, on the way home from downtown. Somehow in the theatre I lost my purse. When I came out I was horrified! To my great relief, a friend of the family and a boarder of ours, Archie Campbell, happened to come along. I asked him if I could borrow some money to buy what I needed to take home. He complied and I went home with my purchase. We did go back into the theatre later and retrieved the purse, much to my relief. My parents never knew about it.

We heard some powerful preaching during those years which made an impact on me. Not only the messages we heard at the camp meetings we attended in the summer, but often my dad's sermons would leave me with an uncomfortable feeling (they called it conviction for sin) and many times I wished I didn't feel so guilty. Though I put on a good front of being a good little PK (preacher's kid), I had a rebellious heart. Jeremiah 17:9 fit me and I knew it: "The heart is deceitful above all things and desperately wicked; who can know it?" It was at a camp meeting, usually held at the Buckingham farm yards in Admiral, which was held in the skating rink in Swift Current, Saskatchewan in 1947, that I confessed my sins and received forgiveness. I knew that I was now headed for heaven, not destined for hell, a place we had heard about in many sermons where there will be "weeping and gnashing of teeth." We didn't get a lot of counseling those days and I don't even remember anyone praying with me. All I remember is that my dear friend, Marion Snowdon, another pastor's daughter, knelt beside me. Even though it wasn't accompanied with a lot of fanfare and no blinding light from heaven, it was a decision that was sincere, one I never regretted. It is interesting to note that I was born in Swift Current and then, twelve years later, having moved six times in between, "born again" there.

Chapter 7:

Junior High Years in Edmonton

In the summer of 1947 we moved to Edmonton, Alberta, just as I was beginning junior high school. That was a very significant move in my life. That summer I had become a Christian and God knew I would have found it hard to survive in the little church with a shortage of Christian friends in Swift Current. The move to Edmonton provided me with a life-long friend, Doreen Flesher. We became inseparable. We arrived in Edmonton late in August just before school was to begin. I hadn't met Doreen but knew where she lived. After walking the three blocks to her house, I knocked at her door the first morning of school and a girl wearing a blue dress and braids in her hair answered the door. I greeted her with, "You must be Doreen," to which she replied, "And you must be Joan."

My beautiful new purple coat, one of the first that was not homemade

It was a friendship like no other I've ever had. A very intelligent girl (though challenged in motor skills) she helped me with homework and as a result I got my best grades in those three years we went to Spruce Avenue Junior High. We did everything together - walked to school, sang, cleaned the church (for 50 cents a week), ate meals, slept at each other's house and vowed that we would be "friends forever." The Anne books were popular at the time and, like Anne and Diana, we called ourselves "kindred spirits." (Many years later she was horrified that we called our first child Elizabeth Ann—without an e!) We were chosen to sing in the Edmonton Youth Chorus, a wonderful experience. We performed at concerts each year and, attired in our beautiful long white dresses, we felt like princesses.

Doreen learned to ride a bike while we were in Edmonton. Although very uncoordinated, with persistence on the part of both of us, she conquered the art and we spent countless hours riding our bikes together. It proved to be our regular Sunday afternoon activity.

It was in Edmonton that I purchased my own bike, an accomplishment I was very proud of. It was a Glider, an Eaton brand which cost somewhere around $25. I bought it on the installment plan for the price of $5.26 per month. Every Saturday I earned $2 babysitting for a family who lived in our neighbourhood. I arrived about noon when the mother went grocery shopping. After her return with her purchases, the couple went out for dinner and dancing until about 2 a.m. Doreen usually stayed with me for the duration. We had fun with the kids, making them supper and enjoying all the good stuff that had been left in the fridge for us to eat, even bottles of pop which was a special treat. I also babysat for a family that lived next door. She informed me that her infant was a Caesarean baby. I had no clue what that meant but later found out in a Guidance class at school when we were encouraged to ask questions. For some reason, I never thought to ask my mother. Something that really shocked me about that family was that they would put beer in the baby's bottle and then laugh when he ended up a little tipsy.

Another one of Doreen's and my many adventures was picking saskatoons. We had to ride the streetcar to an isolated area just past the high-level bridge on the south side of the city. One such day stays in my memory when I had the scare of my life. A young man in uniform came along while we were picking and wanted to know if he could pick into my bucket. He was handsome in his uniform and in my naiveté I was flattered by his attention. For some reason Doreen left me alone and went to a neighbouring farm house to make a phone call. I couldn't believe my ears when my new friend asked me something that I was totally unprepared for. I asked him to repeat it. He refused saying, "You know what I said." He was propositioning me! I was alone and in a panic, thinking he might rape me (although I didn't even know the word then) before Doreen got back. It haunted me for weeks. I dreamed about it and have many times thought how vulnerable I was out there in the bushes alone. Needless to say, we were more careful from then on. I never told my mom about it. The truth is that I didn't feel very close to my mom. I always felt she favoured my older sister. One of the things I resented was that I was totally unprepared for that fateful day when I entered the world of womanhood. It was a great shock to me. All she said was, "Are you sick?" which brought a flood of tears to an unsuspecting 12-year old. I wasn't sick, I was normal!

Doreen and I – kindred spirits!

The three years in Edmonton were formative years for me. Doreen was a very committed Christian and we had many talks about spiritual things. We both desired to live for Jesus. We did many things together, including joining the church. We were very serious about our faith, even fasting regularly once a week, something we were expected to do. She was a fantastic musician who went on to get her ARCT in piano and then her Master's in Music. She was also an accomplished cellist who later played in the Edmonton Symphony.

We were fascinated with weddings in those days. Since there was a United Church near Doreen's home, we would watch for wedding parties on a Saturday and go into the church to observe the proceedings from the back seat. We even planned a double wedding where we hypothetically married each other's older brother. My brother, Rod and her brother, Bruce were best friends. It was complete, even to the colour of the bridesmaids dresses (hot pink and turquoise), the bouquets we carried and the veils we wore on our heads.

One summer when she was on vacation with her family she sent me letters in the mail, each one different from the others. One of them was written entirely on toilet paper. Another had a word misspelled in each line, from the address on the envelope to the end of the letter inside.

Another one of the creative ideas Doreen came up with was a "Season of Devotion," for that period of time between her birthday (January 24) and mine (February 16) when we were the same age. We set down rules for times when we were living in the same place and rules for when we would be separated. It included how many times we would be together, eat together and sleep together. We vowed to always write to each other when our lives went different directions. That was a life-long commitment.

I will never forget the last "Season," the winter of 1980, when I didn't hear from her. I was devastated because I knew that only some kind of tragedy would keep her from our vow. In 1962 I had attended her wedding in Edmonton where she lived at the time. She had married an orthopedic surgeon whose name was also Keith and had had five children, three boys and twin girls who were eight years old.

We hadn't seen each other very often during the years our children were growing up. One summer we met at Harrison Hot Springs in B.C. where we spent a few days together. The twins, Jennifer and Jane were about three or four at the time. Jane had been oxygen-deprived at birth, so was behind her sister in her development. Very unwisely, I referred to Jane as "the twin who doesn't talk," and was immediately chastised by her mother. That was the kind of open relationship we had. I often regretted that we saw so little of each other. I thought that when we were not so busy in retirement we would be able to connect more often. That was not to be.

When I finally heard from her in 1980, she informed me that the cancer which had remained dormant for a few years, had surfaced that winter. Her recent surgery had removed a tumor in her femur. From then on she was confined to a wheelchair. But even in the midst of all that she was going through, she did not forget my 25th wedding anniversary and we received a sheet set that she had ordered from the catalogue. Unfortunately, she didn't get better and died in September of that year. It was a sad time, especially for her husband and children. She was only 44.

I vividly recall my last visit with Doreen in July of that year. By now she lived in Red Deer, Alberta, where she was hospitalized, obviously dying, with lumps on her neck that made it difficult for her to swallow. She was like a China doll so that when I bent over to kiss her, she warned me to be careful. She was in constant pain. Yet she refused to speak of dying and forbade anyone to mention it. She had been very upset by a letter she had received from her missionary cousin that assured her that if she didn't see her again on earth, she would see her in heaven. As a result, her husband screened her letters so that she was never allowed to see a reference to her dying. She wanted so badly to live to see her children grow up and her twin daughters married that she made me promise to pray for her healing. I went away feeling incredibly sad. She wouldn't allow me to enter into her deepest thoughts and emotions. She grieved that her husband, who worked in the hospital, avoided visiting her. It was just too hard. One of the biggest regrets of my life is that I was in Ontario attending a pastors' conference when she died, making it impossible to attend her funeral in Alberta. I felt I never really had closure to that part of my life. And I lost track of the family, never being able to see her kids grow up or go to their weddings. Her husband remarried a woman who was a wonderful mother to the children, especially the twins.

Chapter 8:

My High School Years

When our three-year limit was up in Edmonton, we were on the move again, this time to Winnipeg. It was 1950, the year of the Big Flood. I was going into Grade ten, leaving behind my friends at Spruce Avenue Junior High, especially my best friend. It was terrifying to walk into a school with 1100 students and not know one person in my grade.

I didn't enjoy my high school years because I never felt that I belonged. Since I had only taken conversational French in Alberta in Grade nine, I could not compete with my Manitoba counterparts who had been studying French since Grade seven. Taking a matriculation course without French meant that I was put into Grade 10J while I took all my classes with students in 10A. In my homeroom there were lots of losers - like guys whose only reason to be in school was to play on the rugby team. One of those guys embarrassed me to death when he would sing, "That's what Campbell soups are, M-m good" when he spied me in the hall. I had a few friends, one girl who attended the church and was in a grade ahead of me and one girl that I walked to school with whose dad was a Baptist pastor. We had many theological discussions during those walks. Unfortunately, she later died of breast cancer when she was only in her thirties.

I had a lot of insecurities when I was in my teens and my shyness was sometimes mistaken for snobbishness. Even my dad thought I needed to be friendlier to people at church and reprimanded me. It took a long time for me to realize that I really was an okay person and that God loved me even when I didn't love myself very much. Because of my insecurities and loneliness I turned to eating for comfort and gained quite a bit of weight. That only made my displeasure with myself even greater. However, I did love to bake in those years and always got commendations from dad about the delicious cakes I baked. He also praised me for my ability to iron his shirts to perfection.

Performing in the high school production of the operetta, The Mikado

One of the pleasures of my high school years was the choir and operettas that I sang in. Our school, Daniel McIntyre, had an outstanding choir under the direction of Mr. Pierce and always received high honours in the music festivals. I also took voice lessons during those years and loved my teacher, George Dugard, a Baptist pastor. Singing was one of the few things that I felt I could do well. However, because of my insecurities, I was very sensitive to criticism. One day I was singing the song, "I am amazed that God could ever love me…" when Eveline walked into the room and glibly stated, "So am I!" I was devastated. In looking back, I realize that she probably thought she was being funny but unfortunately, I had trouble seeing the humour.

Mom always took in boarders to supplement the family's income and Winnipeg was no exception. Consequently, there were often extra guests at our table. One year Dad brought home a veteran who had nowhere to go for Christmas to have dinner with our family. Another thing that was common in those days was that out-of-town visitors considered the parsonage as a place that provided free room and board when they came to the city. One such lady arrived at the train station late one evening and called Dad to pick her up and give her a bed for the night. Dad dutifully complied, which necessitated one of us giving up our room, and Mom making up a fresh bed for this (in my opinion) unwelcome guest. I was standing outside the bathroom upstairs the next morning complaining bitterly about this imposition, when the woman appeared, having heard my rather unkind remarks. One part of me was embarrassed and regretted what I said, while another part of me felt that she deserved the retribution. I have been known on occasion, to speak my mind!

We had a rather scary experience one day at school when I was called to the principal's office. I was informed that my sister Shirley (as I recall) had come down with scarletina and we would be sent home immediately and put in quarantine for some time. No one was to leave the house and no visitors were allowed in. It seemed like a long time that we were prisoners in our own house. The only other time that we weren't allowed to go to school was when I was younger and we developed scabies. We had to bath in smelly purple stuff and that wasn't too pleasant a memory either. Such is life!

One of the saddest events of our Winnipeg years was the death of my aunt Mabel, followed in three weeks by the passing of her sixteen-year-old daughter June, both with hepatitis. The loss for Uncle Kenny, Dad's only brother, was devastating. The funerals were held in the Holland area where my dad had grown up. I remember the congregation singing "All the Way My Saviour Leads Me" which ends with the words, "Jesus doeth all things well," and in my heart I questioned that statement.

During my high school years, my interest in teaching drew me into serving as a Sunday School teacher which I did for the five years we lived in Winnipeg. I loved my classes. One of the students was a challenge because she didn't seem to ever really listen to anything I said. She was a twin, born to a couple who had been married for 25 years but who had very little idea how to parent. The twins ran wild, paying no attention to their parents. We spent a good many hours with this family who were always inviting us to their house for meals. The girl, Alfretta, got pregnant as a teenager and became involved in the drug culture. I felt badly that I was never able to reach her. She ended up giving her baby girl to her mother to raise, while she moved on to Vancouver where she died before she was 30 of a drug overdose. The interesting thing about Alfretta's baby was that she grew up to be a Christian woman who married well. It seemed that the grandmother had been given another chance to do it right. An amazing story of redemption!

Another part of that story was the marital problems that these parents had. Mom spent hours talking on the phone to the mother who was suspicious that her husband was seeing another woman. One hair-raising story was of the night she chased him all over Winnipeg in a frenzied attempt to find out what he was up to! In addition, he got into some financial difficulties along the way and they ended up losing their beautiful home, along with their grand piano. A few years later we found out why our family had been invited to their home so often. In actuality, the gentleman was infatuated by my mom. This became evident when Dad had gone to Brazil and he showed up at Mom's door, immaculately dressed, inviting her out for dinner. During the meal he reached over to touch her hand, suggesting that she must be missing her husband. She was, but she certainly wasn't looking for affection from any other man! It was such a shock to her so that from then on she avoided his attentions.

Another teaching experience in Winnipeg was the year we were allowed to have a Vacation Bible School in a school on the south side of the city. We had to travel by streetcar. But it was a wonderful week. One day on the way home we passed a sign that was always up in lights announcing how many days Winnipeg had been fatality free. It said 0 so we knew there had been a death that day. When we got home we discovered that it was a little girl from our Sunday School who had been killed by some road construction equipment that was working on the street outside her house. How sad that was! It was my dubious honour to sing, "Safe in the Arms of Jesus" at her funeral. Her older sister was one of the members of my Sunday School class.

In 1952, my older sister, Eveline married Jim Moore after a whirlwind romance. They met about February and were married August 20th of the same year. Shirley and I were her attendants and Keith, my soon-to-be boyfriend, along with Jim's brother-in-law, Vern Meeds, was also in the wedding party. Jim had no brothers and didn't have any roots in Winnipeg. He had lived in Regina and had left home to join the army when he was quite young. Jim was engaged to a girl in Ontario at the time he met Eveline so he had to return to Ontario to break off the engagement. Eveline cried with relief when he called to give her the good news that he was unattached.

Dad officiated at the wedding but when he asked the congregation to stand (at the wrong time), Eveline burst into tears. As her maid of honour, I had to follow Shirley down the aisle so I had a moment of panic, not knowing what to do. But the bride quickly recovered her composure and the ceremony went on without another hitch.

That was the summer I met the man of my dreams, though at

Handsome Keith

first I didn't recognize him as that. Keith Taylor had been one of Eveline's many boyfriends and I always said I didn't want any of my sister's cast-offs. I had enough of that since I was young with the clothes that were often hand-me-downs. Keith and his dad made a trip into Winnipeg in February of 1952 to sell cattle affected by a devastating disease. Mom asked Eveline if she was going to spend the evening with Keith but she had a date with Jim and in no uncertain terms declared that she was not going to "sit around talking about the hoof and mouth disease." So I ended up entertaining him. I had a terrible cold but I remember, between sniffles, spending the evening playing table hockey. It was the beginning of a new friendship. In the summer of that year our paths again crossed at Killarney Camp. That was when our courtship really began. Our first date was going bowling with other young people at our camp. Instead of inviting me himself, Keith sent his sister, Evelyn, to ask me. The reason he gave was that he couldn't go into the girls' dorm where I was staying. But I know the real reason was because he was a very shy guy.

A couple in love, me holding a teddy bear, gift from Keith

I knew all my life that I wanted to be a teacher. I thought that when I graduated from high school in 1953 I would go to normal school (as a teacher training college was called) and prepare for that profession. However, Dad informed me near the end of my Grade 12 year that they didn't have the money to send me. So I got my first job as a typist at Moore Business Forms in St. James following graduation from high school. It is significant that I had taken typing instead of French, a skill that I have used extensively all my life. It is ironic that the only subject I ever failed in school was typing. In Grade 10 we had an undemanding teacher who expected very little of us. But in Grade 11 the teacher was extremely strict and I froze every time she got near. Although my mark at Christmas was 44%, I did manage to pass at the end of the year and acquired a good typing speed. At that time there was no semester system so our courses lasted for the whole year. In June we either wrote exams or had an exception (with at least a 67% average). In Grade 12 we all wrote departmental exams which covered our classes for the whole year. That was very challenging!

My first day of work was June 29, 1953. I don't remember much about my job except that I had a very pleasant supervisor and girls that were fun to work with. All my life I've said I'm not a morning person but I managed to arise early enough to get to work for 8:00 a.m. after an hour-long streetcar ride.

Another interesting experience took place in Winnipeg. My dad, a very trusting person, met a man who made the rounds of some of the local churches, establishing his reputation as an honourable man. One day he appeared at our door with a request that Dad would loan him $208. He had a truck parked outside and said he had had an accident but was on the way to sell a steer. When he sold the steer he would pay the money back. On the back of a tract which, ironically was entitled, "Let no man deceive you," Dad had written the IOU. Of course, the man never returned. When Dad inquired about him at the police station he was told that he had a record as long as your arm. The problem was, he hadn't really stolen anything—the money had been given to him. But at the police station they told Dad that the man owned some furniture that was in storage. If Dad wanted to get a piano that he owned he could get whatever he could out of it as partial payment. Consequently, we had two pianos in our house for a while, one of which Dad sold for $175 so it wasn't a complete loss. Another lesson learned.

One of the changes in my life in Winnipeg was the accumulation of glasses. I had suffered with near-sightedness for some time but finally it was serious enough for my parents to realize that I needed them. Because money was in short supply, it was a family friend, Mrs. Willows who paid for my first pair. A vivid memory for me of that time is seeing a streetcar passing on Main Street, many blocks from where I was standing.

Chapter 9:

Changes in my Lifetime

From the time of my birth until now, as I have just celebrated my eightieth birthday, I have seen many huge changes in the world. When I was growing up our family had no TV, indoor plumbing, running water, computers, or even electricity until I was twelve. We never flew on a plane, ate in restaurants or stayed in motels. When we traveled we stayed in cabins which were very primitive with wood stoves and few conveniences. When we traveled by car in the winter time we took heated bricks to keep our feet warm since the cars had very inadequate heaters, one of them being the Austin. The most common means of transportation other than cars was the train. One of my favourite train rides was to visit my friend who lived on a farm only a few miles away from where I lived. In fact, I am still fascinated by trains and would love to take one of those train trips across Canada and through the Rockies (one of the items on my "bucket list").

Today's youth can hardly imagine a world without computers, cell phones or other technological devices. I have to admit that outdoor biffies were never my favourite places (with catalogue pages instead of toilet paper, Christmas time being the exception when we had the much softer wrappings from the oranges!), having an icebox instead of a refrigerator was sometimes an inconvenience (like when we'd been away and the water from the melting ice was all over the kitchen floor), cooking with a wood stove made it hard to keep the oven at a consistent temperature, coal oil lamps didn't give a very bright light and party telephone lines created stress when other people heard your news as soon as you did! The irons that preceded the electric iron left much to be desired. Having to be heated on the wood stove, they kept cooling off. The gas iron which came later was not much better. It scared me half to death when it would shoot out flames.

Some speak of the "good old days" but I must say I prefer the modern conveniences – being able to type on a computer where you can correct your mistakes is a big improvement over a typewriter, even an electric one. The microwave oven and dishwasher are among my favourite modern conveniences, to say nothing of the fridges, stoves and freezers which are a must in any kitchen. Automatic washers and dryers make doing laundry so easy – a great improvement over the washing machines with wringers, then hanging the clothes outside to dry, especially on frigid winter days. Or, after bringing them inside, drying them on a "clothes horse" when everything would be stiff as boards.

I remember the day I saw my first TV. It was in a store window in Winnipeg when I was about 15. I was fascinated! Seeing Liberace playing the piano with his fancy clothes and candelabras gracing the piano was a sight to see. Of course, it was in black and white. We never owned a TV as long as I was home. We bought our first one in 1963 when President Kennedy was shot and we wanted to follow the events during that time of mourning.

While there were difficult things about those "olden days," there were also good things. I believe that the sense of community was greater, as neighbour kids created their own fun without the aid of technology. Games, both indoor and outdoor, helped pass many hours as family and friends played together.

In fact, games have always been something I have enjoyed, whether outdoor or indoor table or group games. My fascination with the game of Scrabble began about the time we got married. We bought our first game in Seattle for $1.88, on sale because the box was damaged. I have played many games since and my fascination has grown over the years, to the point that I play in two Scrabble clubs each week and have competed in many tournaments over the past twenty years. To say I am competitive is an understatement! But I have been trying, without great success I must confess, to become a gracious loser. It's so much more fun to win! Though Keith doesn't share my love for Scrabble, he likes other games and we have friends that we regularly get together with to play Wizard and Five Crowns. There was a time that Rook was our favourite game, but that has been replaced. At Seattle they used to call Rook "Free Methodist Poker!" It was the game to play during exam week to relieve the pressure. Games are still good stress relievers.

Chapter 10:

The Influence of Legalism

The story of my life would not be complete without a mention of the legalism that characterized the church in my growing-up years. It made life difficult for me, especially living in the parsonage. My dad was so dedicated to the Lord and the church in those years that he accepted all the restrictions that the church put on him, and that included his family. At times these things were very hurtful. I was the one girl in the family who was born with naturally straight hair and often wished to have beautiful curls like my sisters, instead of braids which were my lot. I remember the day at camp when a lady from the area took me home and put waves in my hair. I went back to the camp feeling like a beautiful princess. But when Dad took one look at me he was upset and in no uncertain terms told me to comb my hair out. I know that he never intended to hurt me and he really did love me but at that moment of devastation, that was hard to believe.

Another vivid memory I have was my father's reaction to a lovely yellow straw hat that I purchased for $1.00. At that time we all wore hats to church. On Easter we proudly dressed up in new clothes, hats and gloves. Even our girls wore hats when they were little. But this particular hat was problematic because it had yellow flowers on it and that was "superfluous adornment" which was a taboo. My dad told me that he would give me $1.00 if I would throw the hat away - heartbreaking! The Bible verse that governed all such restrictions came from I Peter where it says, "Your beauty should not come from outward adornment, such as braided hair and the wearing of gold jewelry and fine clothes. Instead, it should be that of your inner self, the unfading beauty of a gentle and quiet spirit, which is of great worth in God's sight." Further confirmation came from the Apostle Paul's letter to Timothy, "I also want women to dress modestly, with decency and propriety, not with braided hair or gold or pearls or expensive clothes, but with good deeds, appropriate for women who profess to worship God" (1 Timothy 2:9). I have come to understand these verses to mean that what truly makes a woman beautiful is not what she puts on the outside, but on what is inside. I loved the story of Billy Graham's wife, Ruth who was advised by her husband not to wear makeup and jewelry on a visit to England. Billy told her that they might not understand, to which she replied, "Then I'll shed a little light on their understanding!"

A Christian woman was considered "worldly" if she wore any makeup or jewelry, expensive or not. It was a restriction that lowered my sense of self-worth since in the early 50's you really stood out from the others during a time when bright red lipstick was popular. Another of my dad's arguments was that the Bible declared that wicked Queen Jezebel "painted her face." What teenager wants to be different? I certainly didn't. I felt that it was unfair that Christian girls had to look "different" while the guys blended in. One Friday night when I was leaving for youth group (I was the leader), I came downstairs wearing a red neckerchief, in fashion at the time. My mother looked at me and said, "You shouldn't wear that bright scarf. Remember you must be an example." That made no sense to me and I considered the rebuke totally unjustified, but I took it off. Many times since, I have thought about all the beautiful red flowers that God created to dress up his creation. Of course, we were forbidden to attend movies or dances and I accepted that without questioning. It was part of the cost of discipleship. The only dance I ever attended was when I was in Grade eight. Mom and Dad were away and a missionary couple were staying with us. I told them I was going to a school "party" which in reality was a dance. I found it so much fun and probably would have gone again if Doreen, who had a more tender conscience, hadn't said she wouldn't go. My only other experience of dancing was in 2014 when I danced with our grandson at his wedding. Another significant moment in my life. And I didn't even feel guilty!

I had a strong desire to please God - and my dad - during those years. But life could have been more pleasant without all the rules and regulations we were expected to uphold. I never felt that I quite lived up to all of Dad's expectations. When he would see a plain, young woman with long hair and no makeup, he would make a comment about how beautiful she looked. He would have preferred that we not cut our hair. It wasn't until I was 50 that I finally heard Dad express his approval of me. He was visiting us in our home in Eyebrow when he came into the kitchen and said to me, "Joan, you are a wonderful woman." I felt like I stood ten feet tall!

There have been many changes in the church from the legalism of the past. Gone are the days when you couldn't "smoke, drink or chew, or run around with those who do!" While smoking is still unaccepted, it being mainly a health issue, there is still some difference of opinion on social drinking. Prohibitions on movie-going, dancing, wearing makeup and jewelry have all been lifted. Even the way people dress to go to church has completely changed. I still like to dress up on Sunday, as do many women, but men wearing ties are few and far between. Some of these changes we have struggled with but we know that things change, whether we are ready for it or not. In all these situations, our part is to show grace toward those who do not share our views.

Chapter 11:

Dad's Desire for a New Venture Led to Brazil

During Dad's pastoral years in Winnipeg, he spearheaded the construction of a new church as well as a building to accommodate the needs of the Western Holiness Bible School which had moved from McCord to Winnipeg in the fall of 1953. The new building included dining area and classrooms in the basement, faculty housing on the main floor and dormitory space for girls and guys in the upper level. Upon the completion of these projects, Dad needed a new challenge, so, without Mom's knowledge or approval, he applied to the mission board for pioneer missionary service in Brazil. Mom was quite sure that because Dad was 50, he would not be accepted. However, that was not the case. On July 21, 1953 he left to scout out the possibilities of establishing a mission work in the interior of Brazil. Mom was devastated and the ensuing year was not the happiest one in my memory, to say the least.

SOUTH AMERICA

PASTOR AND MRS. MURDO CAMPBELL AND ROSS

During Dad's absence the family lived in a home which Dad had previously purchased as a revenue house. That is quite a story!

The house, located on the Red River, had been significantly damaged by the flood in 1950 so Dad purchased it at a very reasonable price. The rent was paid faithfully each month through a rental agency so there was no interaction with the renters. A friend of the family, Sel Belsher, who took an interest in the house and made periodic visits there, noticed something suspicious about the place on one of his visits. The curtains on the windows were discoloured and there were no signs of life around the establishment. One evening when Sel approached the windows of the house to check it out, he detected a very strange odour. To his consternation, he concluded that he was smelling alcohol and that the place was being used by bootleggers. He spied out the comings and goings of the renters for a few days and reported his suspicions to the police. The men were apprehended and we were left with a very dirty, foul-smelling house to clean up. The house was at a prime location for bootlegging because of the accessibility of the river in which to deposit the mash. I remember taking time off school in June of 1953 to wash walls and help prepare the house for occupancy. My sister Shirley who was in high school, my little brother, Ross who was only about nine, and I moved in with my mother when Dad left for Brazil. I lived there only one year after high school, then went to Bible College where I shared a dorm room with my high school friend, Wilma Fox.

I had this photo taken especially for Keith

That was a good year. During most of the two years that Keith and I had been dating we rarely saw each other and almost never phoned. This long-distance relationship was maintained by letter-writing. Our letters expressed how much we missed each other and longed for the time when we would not have to say good-bye. That third year, the year before we were married, it was exciting for us to be together. We saw each other every day, ate our meals and did dishes together (our gratis assignment), and played many games of ping pong, our main source of entertainment. He was a hard-working student, pursuing biblical studies, in preparation for ministry so we also spent a few hours studying. I tried to teach him how to sing bass that year but decided that was not his gift. He always encouraged me in my musical interests. The enrolment was small at the college so the guys and girls were housed in the same building. My heart went pit-i-pat when I heard his footsteps on the floor above, the building being far from soundproof.

Another plus for that year was being with my dear friend and fellow-student, Doreen. She was pursuing her ARCT in piano so practiced four hours a day. She could never have done it if she hadn't been able to get her courses with very little studying. When we took an IQ test in Junior High, she scored in the genius category. There was one class in which she had a perfect paper but the teacher couldn't bear to give anyone 100% so she got 99%. She was quite enamored by a student named Newell Scharfe and as a foursome we pursued many ventures together. Rules were strict in those days and we were not allowed to date without a chaperone, even though Keith and I had been engaged for several months. We weren't even allowed to sit together in church, except for the Sunday before our wedding. One of our fun pastimes was roller skating, which was the closest to dancing we could get. I loved it. We didn't eat out very often but when we did it was very special. Fortunately my mom lived in Winnipeg so we could escape there when we needed some time alone. Keith graduated in early April and we were married on the 15th. Our plan was to further our education at Seattle Pacific College in the fall.

Chapter 12:

Another New Beginning-- Marriage

How would I describe Keith, the man I was about to marry? He was a man of integrity through and through. Sometimes I thought he was a little too honest, telling people things that I didn't think they needed to know. Whenever we arrived at a border crossing he got incredibly nervous, I'm not sure why except that he was very conscientious and wanted to do everything right. This goes back to childhood when he would feel guilty for "stealing" raisins (one of his favourite treats). His mother always told me what a good boy he was. There was never a time when he would hurt anyone deliberately. Even when he was at the School of Agriculture in Saskatoon the year after high school he had a reputation for honesty. Some misdemeanour had taken place after which one of the guys made the remark, "Go ask Taylor, he'll tell the truth."

He was also a very committed Christian, which was a must. We both went into marriage with the assurance that we were doing the right thing, that we would follow our dreams together and build our home on the solid foundation of faith.

Of course, he was not faultless. My biggest struggles have been over the differences in our attitude toward money. He believed it was for saving while I thought it was for spending! That surfaced early in our relationship when I was disappointed that he didn't get me a diamond engagement watch, as I had suggested, since we were not allowed to wear diamond rings. But I conclude that a relationship survives when you accept one another for who they are, warts and all. He has always been generous with me and never minded spending money on clothes so I can look good. His love and support of me has never wavered.

Our wedding day was fairly mild and windy. I thought everything was in order on the morning of the wedding but discovered that my sister's veil which I had borrowed had come back from the cleaners full of holes. We didn't have much money those days so I didn't consider buying another one. A logical solution was to go to Malabar's, a costume rental place, and rent one. Because the room was dark and dingy, I couldn't see that the veil was filthy. However, when exposed to the light it became apparent that I must take it back and have it cleaned. All of this travelling was in my sister's current boyfriend, Dave Pickering's RCMP car. He was not supposed to have passengers so I ducked down every time we saw another police car! Otherwise, the wedding day was a great memory.

In my diary I described this day as the Happiest Day of my Life!

Only fifty guests attended the wedding because of our financial situation. My sister, Shirley was my only bridesmaid. The groomsman was Keith's long-time friend, Allan Green who later married his sister Evelyn. Dad had just gotten home from Brazil so he was able to give me away. That was a special moment. Rev. E.H. Childerhose, beloved Bible teacher and family friend, officiated. I sang "The Wedding Prayer" with my dearest friend, Doreen at the piano. My other girlfriends were the servers at our sit-down turkey dinner reception, which my mother prepared. The MC was supposed to be Dr. Ross Willows but he, an obstetrician, was called away to deliver a baby. So a family friend, Selwyn Belsher, filled in the gap and did an excellent job. His wife, Evelyn, a superb seamstress, had made my dress of brocaded satin. The material cost a total of $25.00. It was a happy event with lots of good jokes and great speeches. The two that stand out were those delivered by our fathers. Keith's dad, a rather quiet man, welcomed me to the family with these words, "I do not feel like I have lost a son; I have gained a daughter." He was a man who deeply loved me and I loved him. My dad's comparison of me with my mom was unique. I was a woman with convictions, I was a good cook.... "just like her mother." My voice teacher, who was a wonderful tenor, sang "The Lord's Prayer" at the wedding and "Because" at the reception.

Our wedding wasn't held until 6:30 in the evening so we were very late getting away from the reception. Unfortunately, Keith had given his attendants the key to our hotel room so when we arrived we discovered that the culprits had placed cornflakes in the bath tub and short-sheeted the bed. We had moments of frustration but they had lots of fun!

We were married just one week after Bible School closing. Keith had graduated from the three-year program and I had completed one year. The months following our marriage were filled with huge challenges. It had been my desire to be married in June when the weather would have been nicer and I would have had more time to prepare. But Keith needed a cook and housekeeper on the farm. He lived and farmed with his brother Don whose wife, Lyla, was in the hospital with rheumatoid arthritis most of that summer. Their little four-year old, Dorothy, was our flower girl and I always thought it was sad that her mother was unable to see her walk down the aisle. She was a happy little girl and so pleased with her new clothes. She reported to the photographer, "I have new panties!"

In retrospect, I wonder why on earth I had arranged to sing at a voice recital the day after our wedding. But my singing lessons were very important to me. It was for that reason that we were married on Friday instead of Saturday. I sang, of all things, "I Know that My Redeemer Liveth," from the Messiah, a very challenging piece. But I survived and thought I had a very understanding new husband.

My initiation to rural life began on the way home from our four-day honeymoon based in an insignificant little motel, "Twin Pines," in Brandon. The April showers came down in torrents, making our trip on Highway #13 a nightmare! We got stuck twice in the dirt roads which were almost impassable. The second time Keith had to leave me in the car and hike to the nearest farm to get a tractor to pull us out. While he was gone I lost my wedding ring somewhere in the car. We did find it later but it wasn't my happiest day! We finally arrived at 1:45 in the morning! We spent the next five months in Don and Lyla's house where we had our small, private quarters upstairs.

So many things were new to me. I kept house, cooked for two men, looked after Don's four and six-year old girls for part of the time, baked bread, canned raspberries, made pickles, tended a garden, washed the cream separator every day (how I tired of that job!), and put up with an ambitious puppy who playfully destroyed my new towels while they were drying on the clothesline! To make matters almost unbearable I suffered from terrible pains in my stomach when Keith was away to a church conference and ended up asking Don to take me to the hospital. I was diagnosed with appendicitis and a kidney infection. By the time Keith got home the decision was made for me to have an appendectomy. So two months after my marriage, I was stuck in the hospital in a ward with a woman who spoke only French in a community where I knew no one. It was one of the loneliest times of my life. Furthermore, I missed my Grade 8 singing exam for which I had been preparing for months and never did take it. I got a telegram from my parents with Romans 8:28 on it – and to this day I don't know how the "all things work together for good..." applied in that situation.

That summer we were in charge of the children's work at Killarney Camp so it turned out to be one of the busiest summers of my life! Keith worked long hours – sowing the crops, cultivating, picking rocks, forking hay and at the end of the day, milking cows. Besides that, he painted the barn in his spare time! However, it wasn't all work. We did have some pleasant times visiting friends and family in the community. We attended a family wedding shower for one of Keith's cousins who had been married that summer. They had had a very large, lavish wedding with many attendants. The pictures were beautiful; our wedding seemed so small, by comparison. But sadly they ended up divorcing a few years later. In the nearby village we attended the church which was supplied by a lady United Church minister. I also helped with the Vacation Bible School that was held there in the hall. On September 11, we boarded the bus to embark on the next phase of our life's journey - Seattle Pacific College in Seattle, Washington.

Chapter 13:

Adventures at Seattle Pacific College

We thoroughly enjoyed our three years at SPC. One of the things I quickly got used to there was my new name, writing it dozens of times when registering for classes. At first I signed my full name, Barbara Joan Taylor. But I would get called Barbara in class which wasn't me. So I began signing B. Joan Taylor, which is my signature to this day. However, on official forms like passport and Health card you have to have the full name. I'm getting used to being called Barbara at medical appointments. I learned my lesson big time when several years ago I was in the Regina airport waiting to fly to Toronto. I had inadvertently left my wallet at the lunch counter. When they called Barbara Taylor to come to the Information, I ignored it and even remarked that someone had a name like mine! When we got to Toronto and there was no wallet in my purse, I realized that it was me they were calling! How embarrassing. I vowed that would never happen again. Now I answer to both names.

We stayed in two different third floor apartments on campus in Seattle. The first one was small with a very tiny kitchen and one other room -- our living room, study and bedroom. The bed was one of those on hinges that magically appeared at bedtime from inside a closet. Our second apartment, just across the hall was big by comparison -- two rooms plus a kitchen. Our large bedroom easily accommodated two desks so that was where we studied. The fifty-six steps up to our apartment kept us in shape those days. We certainly made every effort not to forget anything when we left for our 8:00 a.m. classes! Just outside our kitchen window was a beautiful cherry tree, a variety that didn't grow in Saskatchewan. How I loved those pink blossoms in the spring! We both attended school full-time and had jobs on campus part-time. I worked 14 hours a week in the Registrar's office, a position which turned into full time in the summer. I enjoyed my work and the girls in the office became my friends. Keith started out working on campus (for $1 per hour) but in the second year he bought a lawn mower and developed his own business which continued from February into the fall. He also worked at a cedar shakes mill during the summers. We were busy but happy. We had several couple friends, some of whom we still keep in touch with. We attended a lively church with a wonderful pastor. We loved the beauty of the Seattle area - so many things to see and do.

One of the advantages in being in Seattle during those three years was that we were so close to Vancouver where my sister Eveline and her family lived, as well as Keith's brother Glenn and his family. We went to B.C. for most of the special occasions, since Mom and Dad were in Brazil during that time. The Christmas of 1956 we drove with Glenn, Dolores and their boys to the Prairies to spend the holiday with the Taylors. That was a memorable winter trip! It was a blessing to have family so close. Shirley graduated the same year we did, from Vancouver General Hospital where she became an R.N. She was so beautiful in her white nurse's uniform and red roses! All of the family attended the New Westminster Free Methodist Church at that time where Donald Bastian (later to become bishop) was the pastor. We enjoyed being part of that very alive congregation when we went to visit.

One of the extra-curricular activities I engaged in was the SPC Chorale, a singing group that gave me many great experiences. We had singing engagements around the State and the members of that group became friends. The school acquired an old army base at Cape Casey on Puget Sound that provided a place to go for different activities. I took a camping course with a friend which we put into practice when she and her husband joined us for a camping weekend at Mount Rainier. We slept in a tent and cooked our food over an open fire. It was early in the year and the snow was many feet high. Another experience at Mount Rainier was when Keith's brother, Martin and sister, Evelyn came to visit us. We took a picture of the flowers (which we had planted) in the snow! That was quite an experience for two young people from the Prairies. Seattle was a pretty formidable place to drive, lots of very steep hills. I had never gotten my driver's license while we lived in Winnipeg and I certainly didn't want to start there!

The day before graduation they always have an ivy-cutting ceremony where the ivy is cut between the students, symbolizing leaving the sacred halls of learning. Ours was cut between us but we would remain together, not as most students who stood side by side. I was very proud on graduation day to celebrate with my family. My parents, just home from Brazil, were able to attend as well as Mom's mother and sister. I still remember the comment made by my Aunt Ada, who had a great sense of humour. When comparing me graduating from college with her only daughter, she declared that her daughter's only accomplishment was having two babies in one year! Actually I thought that was quite an accomplishment!

A very proud moment for us as we graduated together.

One thing that changed for us in those days was our legalistic viewpoints. It was hard to believe that Baptist women could look so "worldly" and still be spiritual! The college at that time was fairly small, 1400 students, and we were amazed at some of the professors who called all the students on campus by name. I got my

Bachelor of Arts in Education - fulfillment of a dream. I did my practice teaching in a Grade four class which I thoroughly enjoyed and my secondary education teaching Grade 10 Spanish, a challenging experience. Keith earned his degree in Missions.

All of our lives we had responded to a call to serve as missionaries and went to college to prepare for that vocation. Many of our friends had the same intention and we were active in the Foreign Missions Fellowship where we met some quality people. One year we, along with four fellow-students, enjoyed a memorable drive across the country in our 1956 Chev station wagon to Urbana, Illinois for a missionary convention. Well-known speakers like Billy Graham and Donald Grey Barnhouse challenged us with powerful messages. That was a highlight in our lives, both the trip (even the flat tire!) and the conference. It was one of the few years that Christmas was almost forgotten. However, a missionary career did not become a reality for we were turned down by the Mission Board, largely because of Keith's "D" in Spanish. They concluded that he wouldn't be able to learn the difficult Chinese language, for we had applied for service in Hong Kong. I'm sure it was the right decision but at the time we were quite disappointed. However, it did not deter us from full-time ministry since Keith had received a call to preach at a missionary convention at the age of 21 and intended to be obedient to that call. I always had said that I did not want to marry a minister or a farmer but in actuality Keith was a combination of the two. However, my love for him and commitment to serve the Lord won the day. He never lost his love for the rural lifestyle. We invested 32 years in pastoral ministry, mostly in rural communities.

We had an eventful trip back to Saskatchewan from Seattle, camping with our little pup tent. Our station wagon was full to the roof with everything we owned. Going through what was known as the Big Bend highway in B.C. was incredibly winding and rough. The mosquitoes were so ferocious that when we stopped to go to an outdoor rest area, it was almost impossible to stay long enough to do our business. We ended up in a motel overnight because you couldn't be outdoors. Needless to say, we were glad to be home. The exciting event of that summer was the marriage of Keith's sister Evelyn to his best friend, Allan Green. Although the July day was beastly hot, the wedding was lovely. Keith was best man and I sang, wearing the pretty mauve dress I had worn as a bridesmaid at Eveline's wedding.

Chapter 14:

Welcoming our Firstborn – a Daughter

Our three years at Seattle allowed me time to be out of the fishbowl where I felt that I was no longer being scrutinized by parishioners or trying to live up to my parents' expectations. So, ready or not, I was back to the fishbowl again! Our first ministry appointment began at McCord, Saskatchewan, the same town where my father had pastored when I was a child. But by the time we got there, the church was barely alive. Most of the people had moved away and the ones who still lived in the community had little interest in spiritual things. But there were a few bright spots in that rather discouraging year. We held Sunday School in the morning, a service in a schoolhouse 17 miles away in the afternoon and another in McCord in the evening. We had only four people in McCord that we could count on but they were among the best people on earth. The few attendees at the Meyronne afternoon service were also wonderful people who loved and supported us. The Little family were part of that congregation. Eveline and I had become friends of the twins, Jean and Joan, a friendship which has spanned many years. Jean became a missionary and Joan a pastor's wife. They are, like me, in their eighties.

Others in the area had been touched by the church and still appreciated a pastoral call. We had many enjoyable times there. The townspeople were friendly and accepting. We had a good CYC (Christian Youth Crusaders) where we were able to get to know some of the town kids. I still use a recipe that one of the girls in my cooking class had given me. Our farewell a year after our arrival was a memorable event where almost the whole community met in the town hall and gave us a wonderful send-off. For over fifty years, we kept in touch with people that were part of our lives that year, though now there are very few left.

When Christmas time came that year, we knew that we couldn't travel and be with family since the due date for the arrival of our firstborn was December 26. We endeavoured to make the best of it and, looking back, we remember that year as one of the best Christmases ever. We had three invitations to people's homes. We had developed a friendship with the United Church minister and his wife so had invited them for dinner. I still remember that she brought trifle for dessert, something I had never even heard of. I had grown up with mince pie and Christmas pudding. They had two young children very close together (one conceived while she was still breast-feeding) so they were able to give us some up-to-date advice about child-rearing. One of their warnings was not to expect a thing of beauty when our firstborn would arrive on the scene!

However, when Elizabeth Ann (Beth) made her appearance January 9, 1959 we were completely overwhelmed! To us, she was gorgeous! She weighed in at 6 lb. 9 oz., a perfect size. We didn't know much about labour (I had no access to pre-natal classes in those days) so when I began to experience pain at 4 a.m., we thought we should get to Mankota, about 20 miles away. We arrived at the 10-bed hospital at about nine but nothing much happened all day. It got to be close to 8 o'clock in the evening when the doctor, thinking it would be a long time yet, invited Keith to his house next door to play pool. But in

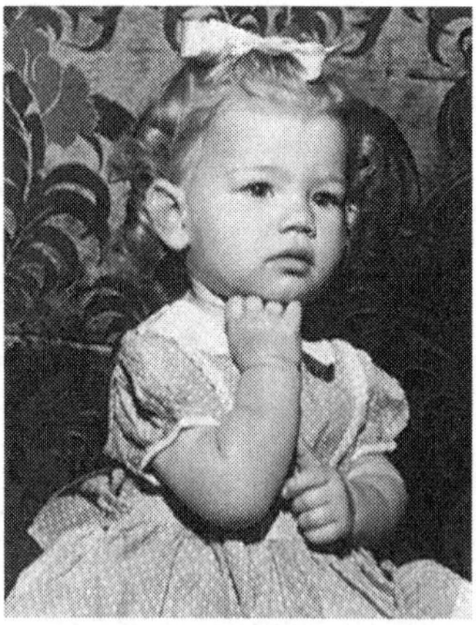

Our adorable little curly-haired girl, Elizabeth Ann

my case, when things started to happen, they quickly escalated. The nurse finally called the doctor to return to the hospital because it was getting urgent, so back they came. Beth arrived at 11 p.m. In reality, I could have been prepped a little earlier and the doctor apologized that he hadn't gotten there sooner! Now I understand where Keith experienced his first interest in pool!

Life was not easy with our firstborn. I tried unsuccessfully to nurse her and ended up staying in the hospital for ten days in order to adjust her formula. That was a lonely time because Keith didn't come to see me every day and no one else was allowed to visit. Two ladies from the church came to the hospital but they could only greet me from the door. Only the patient's mother could enter the room and mine was far away. I wasn't allowed out of bed, not even to go to the washroom!

When I finally was released from the hospital, my mom had arrived but it didn't go very well because Beth, not a happy baby, cried a lot. She was unable to handle the formula so threw up almost every time she was fed a bottle. It was most distressing. My mother was not home very long from her stressful experiences in Brazil and her nerves were frayed. The ladies of the town planned a surprise baby shower for us which was also difficult for Mom. While I was blissfully having a nap upstairs she was making sure that the house was immaculate and ready for our guests. It was a wonderfully affirming event for me. Beth got everything she could ever need, including 11 dresses, and I was thrilled! When I put on those beautiful clothes, it was like dressing my own little doll. After about 10 days, Mom confessed that she felt like Keith and I were taking sides against her. In reality, everyone was exhausted since Beth had her days and nights mixed up and none of us was able to get a decent sleep. In desperation, when we took the baby back to the hospital to get her formula adjusted (again), Mom felt it was time for her to leave. We found out that the baby's formula (one oz. of Carnation milk to two oz. of water) was too weak. When it was changed to the opposite combination, she thrived!

Those were the days when we all used cloth diapers. With no plumbing, the dirty ones had to be scraped, rinsed and used again. Ugh. All the ladies of the town hung out their wash early Monday morning. Mine was lily-white compared to my neighbour's who had three sets of twins and a single under the age of five. I never had disposable diapers until years later when Marilou was born. Then they were only used when we went on trips.

One of the significant events of that year was the union of the Holiness Movement Church, to which we belonged, to the Free Methodist Church. It became official on January 1, 1959. So I have always said that Beth was born a Free Methodist! It brought quite a few changes into our lives, among them meeting many new, wonderful people and experiencing a wider selection of churches in which to minister.

One of my most disappointing experiences during our year in McCord was when my dad invited me to be the soloist for evangelistic meetings he was holding in Estevan. Keith could not agree to this because he felt he couldn't manage without me. So I declined the offer. I felt resentful about it for quite awhile because I felt it was selfish of him. I loved to sing and felt it would have been such a wonderful experience to team up with my dad. Another time during that year, when we went to a missionary convention where my parents were speaking about their Brazil experiences, they invited me to go back with them to Winnipeg, offering to pay my bus fare home. Keith was unhappy but I decided to go anyway. I reasoned that I had hardly seen my parents since their return from Brazil. But I was miserable the whole time. I learned some lessons during those experiences—that it was necessary to come to an agreement about decisions we made and that compromise is the best way. I also had to understand that my husband needed my support in his new pastoral role. For us, pastoring has always been a team effort and I have been content with that.

Chapter 15:

Another Challenge -- the Broadview Indian Mission

When Beth was six months old, in August of 1959 we moved to Broadview, Saskatchewan in order to give Lloyd and Bessie Robertson, missionaries to the Indians (now referred to as aboriginals or First Nations people), a furlough. They had worked "in the soul interest of the Indians" for ten rather thankless years. While Lloyd was clearing the land to build the church and parsonage on the edge of the reserve, he lost his leg in a tractor accident. In the sixteen months we were there we often found the work challenging. But it was a place to learn some good life lessons. One plus factor about Broadview was that we were only an hour and a half from Keith's home. We often took refuge there when we needed a break. Another bright spot was a Mennonite couple, Ernie and Mary Dyck, who worked in Broadview, he at a bank and she at the Coop store. They were a wonderful couple, teaching Sunday School and loyally supporting us. They had a love for the Indian people and later went to Africa

Our family as we began our work at the Broadview Indian Mission

as missionaries. We were able to get close to a few of the people but with most there was some reserve.

One of my duties was to prepare for monthly clothing sales which became a source of great frustration to me. People would come between sales and want to get clothes for some special occasion. I remember in the spring one of the ladies came, requesting that I search for clothes for her children for Easter Sunday. After I rooted through the many boxes looking for just the right outfits, they took the clothes, then ended up attending another church that Easter! There was always the dilemma of knowing when you should say *No* and when *Yes* when they asked for rides to and from town. We would get phone calls with the message that said, "We're stuck in town" (10 miles away). Keith made it a policy that he didn't make special trips unless they had been released from hospital or there was some other emergency. On one occasion we took a young unmarried woman to the hospital as her baby was about to be delivered.

The day that we shared with an Indian couple the baptism of our children

We had come home from college with a 1956 Chev station wagon which could hold a good number of people – too many, we quickly decided. It had been wonderful for the trip home from Seattle because we were travelling with all our earthly possessions and needed the space. But when it seemed wise to get a smaller vehicle, Volkswagen was the logical choice because of its ability to handle the winter roads, which were not paved. When we went to pick up boxes of used clothing that people sent, we were amazed at how many boxes could be jammed into that little car. It could also hold an amazing number of people.

Keith had an interesting experience when he went to officiate at a wedding and discovered that the couple had not acquired a license. The banquet had been prepared—and they could really put together a wonderful meal—but there was no wedding. Later he went back and finished the job. Not that weddings were a necessity for many of them. They declared that things went better when they just lived together. When they got married they seemed to be more insecure in their relationship.

One of the sad events of our time there was the death of a baby. I will never forget the burial ceremony. When the little casket was put into the grave the family and friends began to loudly wail and cry, something I had never experienced. It reminded me of what you might see in a pagan culture. Then they threw a blanket into the grave to cover up the casket.

The work ethic of the people was a thorn in Keith's side. When they saw the garden he tenderly cared for they would say, "You're lucky to have such a good garden." When Keith would ask, "How's yours?" they would answer, "Full of weeds!" It seemed to us that instead of making an effort to give themselves a better life, they spent their time figuring out ways to get more out of the government. We could see that we could not continue to work with them.

Of course, there were some good times too. We had some great prayer meetings in their homes (you just made sure you sat on an unpadded chair so you didn't pick up a bedbug or two) and we enjoyed the lady who cleaned our house. She was a gracious person who was an excellent worker. We had an oil furnace that left a film over everything so washing the walls was a necessary part of cleaning in that house. The water was full of iron so the toilet bowl became badly corroded. Furthermore, the pump for our septic system was always giving trouble. Such were some of the problems of the rural life, but we did have indoor plumbing, a definite plus. I made bread in the wood stove, a new experience for me. I was amazed when it generally turned out well.

We had several members of our families visit us in Broadview. One of those visitors was my sister, Eveline and her family. After we had been at church on Sunday, my niece, Colleen, who was about five at the time, made the observation that she hadn't seen any "Indians" at church. I guess she was expecting tom toms and feathers!

I did enjoy the children and the young girls I taught to play the piano. We kept a little two-year old for a week while her parents were away holding evangelistic meetings. I could have kept her as my own! Some of the people you couldn't help but admire. One lady had a useless arm, yet she worked hard (not the same could be said of her husband) and faithfully walked several miles to church every Sunday. I was glad that we lived near the reserve before alcohol was allowed there because things deteriorated after we left. After that change, the roads were no longer safe.

In 1960, while we were living at Broadview, our conference decided to relocate our camp and buy a property known as Arlington Beach which was located on Last Mountain Lake. It had been owned by the Canadian Sunday School Mission who had operated children's camps there since 1942. There were some old cabins on it, a small tabernacle where meetings were held, a dining hall, a boathouse, dorms for the kids, a building we called the castle and a hotel. A small one-room cabin near a flowing well served as a nurse's station. It was for sale at the cost of $400. I'm not sure where we got the money (our salary was $1800/year) but we bought that cabin to help the church purchase the property.

The land had been formerly owned by the William Pearson Land Co. Steam ships provided transportation on the lake before the arrival of the railroad in the early 20th century. A beautiful hotel, known as the Arlington Beach House, was built in 1910.

We had been involved in directing children's camps for many years, first at Killarney, then Moose Jaw and finally at Arlington Beach. The first few years the camp was only used for children's and youth camps. A highlight of the year was the May Rally for teens. I served as a counselor and choir leader for the youth camps, something I thoroughly enjoyed . One memory stands out when one of the girls snuck out of the dorm sometime in the evening, after I had gone to sleep (I was a good sleeper in those days) and never came back until morning. She had made a pact with a guy to do it together, just to see if they could pull it off. She thought she was very clever when she informed me what she had gotten away with. Fortunately, it was not a guy that the girl liked so no harm was done.

In 1965-66 the tabernacle was moved from Moose Jaw, where the camp had been located for many years, to Arlington Beach. In 1975-76 the new Kinney Memorial Lodge (in memory of Bud Kinney, a faithful supporter of Arlington Beach who was tragically drowned, along with two young sons). The dining room has seating for 300, rooms on two floors for 84 people, two lounges and a staff apartment. Other buildings have been added as the camp has grown.

We sold our little cabin and bought one of the larger original ones from Keith's brother-in-law, Roy Caswell. It was in need of some refurbishing so we put in a washroom and made it quite a comfortable summer home with three small bedrooms.

We have many memories of our years at Arlington Beach in the various camps, ministers' conferences and Ladies Retreats. We had some great speakers and good fellowship. It was truly a place of spiritual renewal and refreshment.

Chapter 16:

It's a Boy!

Our only son, Cameron Ross made his appearance early Monday morning in the Broadview Hospital on October 3rd, 1960. It was a rather urgent trip we made that morning. Waking up at 5 a.m., it wasn't long before I knew this was the day. Still a week before the due date, I hadn't packed a thing. We were thankful that Lloyd was with us at the time (he and Bessie lived upstairs in the mission house whenever they weren't travelling) so he was able to stay with 21-month-old Beth while Keith drove me to the hospital. Keith was back home, barely inside the door, when the hospital called to say that his son had arrived at 7:30. I was thrilled with our little son. He seemed scrawny, only weighing 6 pounds, 6 ounces, the smallest of our children, but I fell in love with him immediately. He was a contented baby right from the get-go. My first attempt at nursing our firstborn, Beth, was so disastrous that I didn't even try with him. He thrived on the canned Carnation milk that was his formula. A very contented baby, he never even attempted to roll over. As a result, it was safe to leave him anywhere!

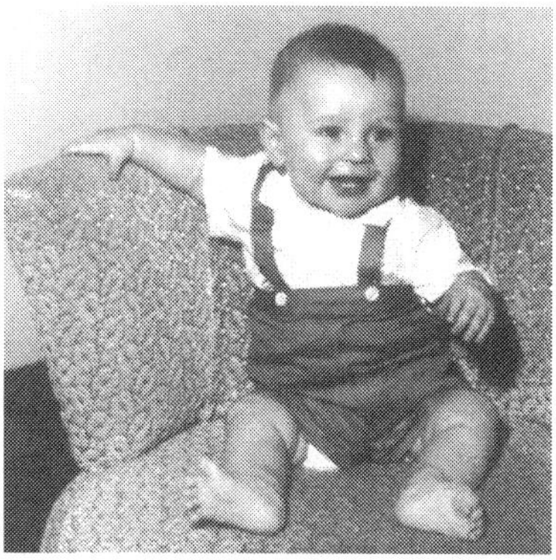

Our happy little son Cameron Ross

My mother was sure that the reason Cameron was so immobile was because he had been brain damaged as a result of my car accident on June 30, 1960, three months before he was born. I wrecked our poor little brand-new Volkswagen but didn't harm myself or my unborn baby in the process. It was a memorable day, one more of the traumatic experiences of our Broadview tenure. I was on the way to take Beth to see the doctor (unbeknown to me, she had red measles). A 15-year old girl was with me, holding Beth on her knee in the front seat (no car seats at that time). Her parents had come from Ohio to work at the Mission and her mom was up on a ladder painting when she got this sudden urge to pray for us on our way to town. She descended the ladder, got down on her knees and asked God to protect us. The car rolled two-and-one-half times in a rather deep ditch but no one was hurt. In looking over at Beth, I hit gravel on the side of a freshly graded road, turned the wheel quickly (not knowing anything about the direct steering in the VW) and lost control. It all happened so fast but I do remember saying as we were rolling along, "Jesus, help us!" And I'm sure He did. The first thing I saw when I crawled out of our upside-down-vehicle was the back window, which had popped out in the process, with a sign that read, "The Amazing Volkswagen!"

After Cameron's birth on a Monday morning, I was able to be home on Friday so I never missed a Sunday at church. Keith's mom had come to be with the children, but I had to play the piano at the service. Most of the people hadn't heard of our baby's arrival. There was little fanfare over the birth of that baby - no baby showers or special gifts, except from the Dycks who gave us a diaper bag and, of course, family members. One regret I have always had was the fact that we didn't phone my parents to tell them that they had a new grandson. Since he came early, we thought we would send an announcement card in the mail. The problem was that Keith's aunt and uncle (who also lived in Winnipeg) got their card before my mom and dad and they were deeply offended. I can't say that I blame them. What a difference from today when we are in constant communication! When our grandchildren came along, we were notified at the beginning of our daughters' labour pains.

Chapter 17:

On the Move Again!

The day Cameron was one month old and Beth not yet two, we moved to Brandon, Manitoba where the Free Methodist Church was a relatively new work. We were destined to live "underground" in the basement of the church where the windows were coated, blocking our view of outdoors. It distressed me greatly that I couldn't see the children playing outside. We had a fence around the property but it was easy for two little kids to crawl under. The house inside left much to be desired. Mice were frequent visitors in our pantry, which was simply a set of shelves underneath the back stairs. Our family had to use the church's only bathroom which was located at the far end of the basement. In the wintertime, it was a cold walk (or for the children, a run) between our living quarters and the bathroom, for the basement was not heated except on Sunday. Because it was some distance from the furnace, the bathroom was never warm.

Our family at the back door of the Brandon church that was our home

The three years we spent there were some of our most difficult years in ministry because no matter what we did we couldn't seem to make a dent in our community. We tried to have a C.Y.C. to reach the neighbourhood kids but with little provocation or a move by the family, we took two steps backward for every one ahead. The mother of four boys, who for several years had been picked up for Sunday School by a family in the church, called us one day to inform us that they had moved and would be sending their boys to the church on their street. It was like we should be saying, "Thank you for the privilege of having your children." We had made friends with another family with six children and were deeply disappointed when they moved away. They were a beautiful family. We couldn't have survived without one loyal couple, Lorne and Edna Baldrow. They were childless at the time and really loved our kids. Children had much more freedom to explore the neighbourhood then and our little ones would walk the two or three blocks to Baldrow's home to visit quite frequently. They had a TV which was a big attraction. When these good friends thought we needed a night out, they babysat for us.

We lived on the corner of Van Horne Avenue and 18th Street, about three blocks from a little store that was on a busy street. One day the children disappeared and when they arrived home two-and-a-half-year-old Cameron was carrying a loaf of bread. They had no money with them so I knew that there was no way they had paid for the bread. Back we went to the store where I reported the little "thief." The storekeepers hadn't even noticed them. Cameron thought he was doing me a favour!

I don't want to speak unkindly about the dead but one woman in that church made my life very difficult. She had many good qualities and welcomed us into their home any time, insisting that we stay for a meal. I will never forget the piles of newspapers, magazines, and every periodical that she had ever subscribed to that were piled high in her kitchen and every other room in the house. I'm sure she still had the first-ever published *Missionary Tidings* and every subsequent edition. Her sister was a missionary in Africa so she was very missionary-minded. When we had a meal at her home she fussed so much that she never ate a bite until everyone was finished. I decided that she must have enjoyed cold food. She kept a record of every person who attended Sunday School or a church service since the church was started. (Of course, she and her daughter were the founding members.) She gave me no indication that she disapproved of me until one day she complained to my husband that I wasn't friendly when they came into our home for the midweek prayer meeting. The fact of the matter was I was too busy scurrying around to get my little apartment tidied up (the meeting place) and my children prepared for bed! That seemed to me to be unfair. But I believe that people come into our lives for various reasons, some of them to sandpaper us and help to refine us. She contributed to that process.

Another family who helped us keep our sanity was the Borley family who lived about 30 miles from Brandon, at Rapid City. They had five birth children as well as two foster sons. Their youngest son was the age of Cameron. For the first year or two we travelled to Rapid City for afternoon services until there were so few that the church was closed and the Borleys came into town. That was a boost. However, they felt the need to attend another church that was closer and we really didn't blame them. After three years, we felt that it was time for us too to have a change so we requested a move. The Brandon church never got off the ground and finally closed after several discouraged pastors' and people's attempts failed to make it grow. That year I had a diversion in a part-time teaching position where I completed a three-month maternity leave. It was good for me to get out of the house. To earn a little extra spending money was a bonus.

One of my Brandon memories is of a train ride which the children and I took when Mom and Dad were living in Calgary. How we all enjoyed that train ride! There is a lot of freedom on a train. The only scary part for them was looking at the moving ground on those grates that you had to walk over when you went between the cars. Another train trip I took from Brandon was to attend my friend Doreen's wedding in Edmonton. I was the soloist, singing a song that had been composed by one of Doreen's university music professors especially for the occasion. Our Grade nine teacher, Miss Merryweather. attended that wedding. She commented on my shoes, white ones with pointed toes (which were in style), adding the fact that I was a minister's wife, as if it was strange that I would wear stylish shoes!

Another trip I took from Brandon was with my mom and dad to Ontario when Cameron was about two-and-a-half. It was a memorable trip for he learned to whistle and spent a lot of time practicing. On the way we spent one night in a cabin in Ontario which was very cold. In the middle of the night Cam developed an earache and was crying with the pain. Mom and I got up, took a lid off the wood stove, wrapped it up and put the warmth on his ear which eased the pain. It was very difficult for me to see my precious little son suffering. That trip included a visit to Mt. Tremblay in Quebec where my brother Rod was involved in a car race. I met my future sister-in-law, Sylvia (Ross's girlfriend) at that event. She slept with me and I couldn't understand how she could stand to sleep with the monstrous curlers she had in her hair. She certainly looked glamorous the next day!

Another experience during those three years in Brandon when the children were about one and three years old, was when my dad suffered a stroke while he was away preaching in Ottawa. He was hospitalized so my mother, who wanted to be with him, asked me to go to Winnipeg where they were living and manage the household in her absence. Shirley was living at home then, attending University to take a Public Health nursing course, Ross was about fifteen and mom had two boarders who were university students. It was a challenge for sure!

The biggest challenge was with my little brother who was a little rebellious at the time. When I tried to get him to do his homework, he would sit for a few minutes, then decide he needed to go and buy a Coke. One Sunday we were invited to Shirley's fiancé, Alan Hull's, home for dinner. Ross had told me he was going to a friend's place for over Saturday night. He had given me the name of the friend but when I called on Sunday to tell him of our plans, they had never seen him. In actuality he had gone to another friend's place, one of whom my parents did not approve. When I confronted him he had to confess he had lied to me. I couldn't quite figure out why because I didn't know anything about his friends. He had some hair-raising experiences with his rather questionable friends in Winnipeg. At one time I was afraid he'd end up in jail! On one occasion he asked Shirley if he could park her car at the back of the house. But at the corner on the way around the block, he had an unfortunate accident, and that without him having a driver's license. But he turned out to be a wonderful guy -- a good husband, father, brother and citizen.

In 1961 Shirley married Alan Hull, the young intern she had met in the hospital, introduced by a doctor friend of Alan's. He was a member of the closed Brethren in Winnipeg. I was not excited about this marriage prospect because Shirley was a wonderful pianist and singer so it seemed her talents were wasted, since there was no piano in their gospel hall and only men could sing solos. Shirley had just performed in a musical at the university, *Plain and Fancy*, in which she had a leading role. Alan was a very controlling person. Because of some disappointing experiences with him in which I felt he was taking my sister away from me, I became more and more resentful of him. At one point Shirley asked me if I thought "love conquers all," to which I responded in the negative. It took a long time before we had much respect for each other.

Their wedding took place in Winnipeg's Elim Chapel in June of 1961 with 250 guests in attendance, most of whom we didn't know. Shirley was a beautiful bride. A funny thing happened at the rehearsal the night before. My brother Rod was giving her away, since Dad was performing the ceremony. She wanted to have the hymn, "Praise My Soul, Thou King of Heaven," played as she entered the church, instead of the traditional Bridal Chorus. However, Rod objected strongly, declaring that you must have the traditional music. She gave in at the time, then told the organist to play the hymn, as planned. It so happened that Rod didn't even notice! I had the privilege of singing at her wedding. Eveline was disappointed that she wasn't able to be in the wedding, due to an unplanned pregnancy. However, her six-year-old daughter, Colleen was an attendant. In 2011 Shirley and Alan celebrated 50 years of marriage.

Chapter 18

Our Most Exciting Move – to Weyburn

We went to conference that July of 1963 with baited breath. We knew we were moving but we did not know where. Those were the days when you found out your fate at the same time as the people who had gathered to hear the "Reading of the Appointments." When they read us out for Weyburn, we could scarcely conceal our joy. Everything we knew about the church was positive. It comprised a congregation of about a hundred, the result of the amalgamation of the Riverview country church congregation and the one in Weyburn. Most of the people were farmers living in a rural area of southern Saskatchewan where the land was fertile. They were loyal and hard-working, yet they had a fun-loving side to them. The church, which was filled to the front seat was desperately in need of replacement so our biggest challenge became getting a building program off the ground.

The parsonage which was our home was located next door to the church. Three Sunday School classes met there, one in the living room and two in the basement. There was an outstanding group of young people. When they entered the church after Sunday School the only seats left were the first two

The Weyburn parsonage next door to the original church

pews so they all marched up and took their places right under the nose of the pastor. I'm not sure they were all the saints that they appeared to be! But they were good kids. I led them in Bible quizzing and we had many great evenings in our home or theirs having sing-songs for they loved to sing. They always attended youth rallies wherever they were happening and performed skits. One memory is of two Alexander brothers playing pretend bagpipes. Funny!

Our children flourished in Weyburn. There were several young families in the church with children the same age as ours and we enjoyed many good times together. Beth, with a January birthday, finally got to go to school when she was well past six. She loved school and was a very diligent student. I have to admit, we had a few battles along the way since she was our strong-willed child. I recall at a very young age when she didn't want to wear what I had laid out, I gave her several options so that she was the one choosing what she would wear. I have always maintained that being strong-willed is not all bad. Ever the leader, she was not easily influenced. She stood up for her beliefs and her leadership abilities have followed her through life.

In the matter of disciplining children, I must say that Beth was the only one who received any spankings. Occasionally, she would get difficult to deal with and the only solution was her dad using the "rod of correction" which was his hand. It worked every time! For Marilou, the only discipline she needed when she got a little ornery was to send her to her room. She couldn't stand the isolation so it wasn't long before she came out smiling. I know there are no perfect children but Cameron was about as close to perfect as you could get. I don't remember him ever getting a spanking and I don't remember him ever being disobedient. I think there might have been some rebellion inside but it never surfaced.

We had lots of musical talent in the Weyburn church and I was privileged to conduct the church choir, preparing cantatas and contributing to the community Christmas carol festival every year

Our main competition there was hockey. Many *fan-atics* bought season tickets for the games and we had to work around that schedule for many activities, something we had never experienced before (except for some of our Sunday School teachers in McCord where the competition was square dancing!)

When Cam was just a little guy, one of his greatest pleasures was riding his tricycle. He loved to visit the neighbours on the street and whenever he went riding out of the garage and down the street, he was, like Jehu in the Bible, driving furiously! One Sunday after church he rushed to our home next door, hopped on his trike and began to ride in and out among the parishioners who were visiting at the front of the church. To make matters more interesting, he had picked up a cigarette butt off the sidewalk and had it in his mouth when he came in sight. Fortunately, they were a congregation who saw the humour in the actions of the young pastor's son!

Young Cameron with his trusty tricycle in a neighbour's yard

During our Weyburn years from 1963-68, four weddings took place in our family. Ross and Sylvia Bates from Oshawa were married in February of 1966. Rod, who had been married the same year we were in 1955, had been divorced. He married Sandra McLean from Montreal, in September of 1966, a perfect match. Keith officiated at the wedding of his sister, Joyce who married Derrell Rodine in August, 1966. She had lived with us for a short time before her marriage, after graduating from the Regina General Hospital as an R.N. In 1967 Keith also officiated at a lovely ceremony in Spiritwood when his brother Martin married Betty Ann Bowes. Beth performed proudly as a junior bridesmaid.

One of the exciting experiences we had while in Weyburn took place in August of 1966 when we took three teenagers, members of my Bible quiz team, to Winona Lake, Indiana, our church headquarters, to compete on the international level. I had been the teens Bible quiz coach for some time with lots of good competition taking place on the conference level. That was a great trip. The kids were so much fun to travel with. We didn't win but the experience was priceless. All those young people became active members of their church communities.

I had opportunities to teach in various capacities during our five years in Weyburn. I taught a Grade 12 Literature class for adults, a very satisfying experience. The students ranged in age from their 20s to their 50s, one of them being a policeman. He particularly objected to learning Chaucer, in no uncertain terms declaring that it shouldn't be on the curriculum with all the abominable spelling! He reminded me of all the letters of application they received from young people who didn't know how to spell, announcing that they shouldn't be exposed to such indecipherable language with ridiculous spelling. One bright young black man in that class made me feel very proud when he received a mark of 93% in the departmental exam they all had to write at the conclusion of the class. I also enjoyed teaching Typing in an adult night class. For one year I taught Grade 10 English which was not altogether a pleasurable experience or one that I felt I succeeded at. Students in general are not that fond of learning English grammar.

A hurdle we faced that came close to giving Keith ulcers was the conflict over whether we needed to build a new church or not. The church was divided with both sides quite determined that they were right. Some couldn't see that having three Sunday School classes in the parsonage next door was not desirable. Others liked the fact that the church was filled to the doors every Sunday. With a desire to see things change, Keith and three of the laymen took a trip to visit Free Methodist and other churches in the province. They came back declaring that we needed to build, in spite of the opposition. They pooled their resources and came up with the

$3300 payment needed to buy the lots at the edge of the town. We had a very crucial vote that had negative repercussions. It was decided that we would not build without a two-thirds majority. So a vote was taken in which we allowed non-members to vote. We knew that there was one on both sides of the issue. It turned out to be 19 for and 10 against. If non-members had not voted the results would have been 18 for and nine against, a clear two-thirds. The matter was dropped until a later date when it was decided to go ahead with 50% in favour. In spite of the tension caused by the opposition, the building proceeded and it was the beginning of a better future. It was interesting that the person who was most opposed was the first one there, with his sons, to volunteer their services the morning the construction began.

The Weyburn Free Methodist church—original (right) built in 1966, the addition (left) in 1996

It was one of Keith's best years in ministry. He worked hard and the rewards of his labours live on. The Dedication day in 1966 was a thrill. I led the choir in the great old hymn, "And Can It Be" and we had Bishop Boyd, former director of the Light & Life Hour, as guest speaker for the occasion. We will always remember his sermon on the Sunday evening of dedication day when he chose to just "brag on Jesus." That church never looked back. They continued to grow so that in 1996, 30 years after the first church was dedicated, they built a new addition. Today with 300+ attending, they are experiencing a need for further renovations. And, since the spring of 2006, our son-in-law, Jay Mowchenko has been the pastor.

Chapter 19:

Our Prayers Were Answered – a Baby Sister!

One of our happiest family events in our final year in Weyburn was the addition to our family. I had always wanted four children. But my dreams were not being realized. The summer of 1967 we enjoyed a wonderful trip to Expo with Dave and Norma Scott who were formerly members of our Weyburn congregation. Although Dave had left his position as vice-principal of the high school to further his education in Regina, we had remained friends. We left a total of five children with their grandparents while we headed off to Montreal. It was a trip that truly cemented our friendship. On the trip home I was sharing with Norma that I had decided that it must be the Lord's will that we not have more children. She said with great emphasis, "The Lord's will nothing, you need to go to a doctor and see if there's any reason." It so happened that when we arrived home from that trip I was pregnant! In the meantime, our children had been praying for about two years for a baby sister. When I was resigning myself to the fact that our family was complete, they were not fazed and continued

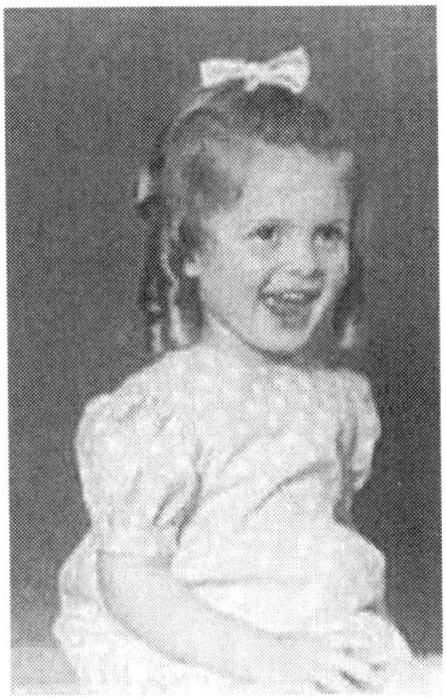

Little Marilou Alice, always a ray of sunshine!

to pray. Then when surprisingly we were expecting, I felt I needed to suggest that they pray for a healthy baby, not specifically a girl. But their prayer did not change. The Lord had no choice but to send us a girl, Marilou Alice, on May 16, 1968. She was absolutely adorable from the moment she entered our world. She had her eyes wide open in wonder and her dad's heart was captivated! He phoned everybody in the church to announce her arrival and there was great joy and excitement. Beth and Cameron were ecstatic. For days before her birth they would burst through the door after school, checking to see if she had arrived yet, before going out to play.

Our fruitful ministry years at Weyburn came to an abrupt end in 1968 when the Stationing Committee decided we should be sent to Roblin, Manitoba to a church that had experienced a split in June. A little more than half of the congregation left at that time so it was not the kind of church that anyone aspired to pastor. I'll never forget the day when Jack Walrath, our conference superintendent, showed up at the door of our cabin at Arlington Beach where the annual conference was held. It was only hours until that memorable moment would arrive for the "Reading of the Appointments." By this time the church had progressed to the point where they would tell you a few hours ahead of time what your fate would be. I was totally unprepared for the shock of that announcement. Those words, "We have you down for Roblin," struck terror to my heart. I didn't want to leave Weyburn, first and foremost, but neither did I want to go to Roblin. Marilou was only two months old so I was emotionally and physically unprepared to move. I loved Weyburn. We lived in a beautiful home (the nicest parsonage we'd ever had), the new church was a great place to worship (the nicest church

Our family, ready to move after five good years in Weyburn

we'd ever had), the kids had good friends in and out of the church, I loved the music I could be part of, I had opportunities for a variety of different teaching assignments, the young people were a delight to work with and take to youth rallies on weekends, and every thought of leaving filled me with great sorrow. When I turned from my seat that day in the tabernacle to face the people after the appointments were read, I could see Weyburn people with tears in their eyes and I was overcome with the disappointment of our new posting. To echo the words of my heroine, Anne Shirley, I was in the "depths of despair!"

To make things worse, the pastor of the Roblin church, who left to help form a new church after the split, came to us with these encouraging words, "I feel sorry for you. Just put in your three years (like a prison sentence) and you'll be able to go somewhere else. There is only one person in that church I have any respect for," and he named her. It was about the most unethical thing I can imagine anyone doing. Keith just turned and walked away from him, not even responding. Thus was our preparation for our new assignment.

Chapter 20:

A Reluctant Move – to Roblin, Manitoba

The day we arrived in Roblin will be forever imprinted in my memory. It was raining - both inside and outside the car! The parsonage was located on the main street, across from the Macleods store, beside the old Free Methodist church which was now used for storage. We drove into the back yard where there was a dilapidated, unpainted garage. On one side of us was a blacksmith shop with all the stuff used for that industry piled around and on the other side, behind the former church, there were rows of culverts. When we went inside the house, it had the worst floors imaginable. We didn't know that the new linoleum they had ordered had not arrived. All the walls were painted a pastel lilac colour. Besides that, our furniture was everywhere. The van had gotten there before we did and everything had been shoved inside in disarray. I felt like turning around and running out of there. The house was small. Because we had to have a crib for Marilou, you could scarcely move in our tiny bedroom where we had only a few inches to spare. One of the little things that bugged me all the time

The Roblin Church located west of the town outside the town limits

we lived in that house was having to climb over Keith to get out of bed. There was absolutely no possibility that the bed could be anywhere other than tight to the wall. The other bedroom was a small one too but big enough for Cameron. The bathroom was a late addition to the house, a room squeezed out of the corner of the already small kitchen. You could barely turn around in there.

Beth loved her open concept upstairs which was one room with low ceilings. It provided a perfect play area for her and her friends. Sometimes I wonder how we did it for we always had room for guests. One year we invited Keith's sister, Evelyn and her family for Christmas. They had three children who joined Beth and Cameron in the upper level of the house. They spent the whole night traipsing up and down the stairs waiting for the time to open the gifts. One Christmas when Marilou was very young, she got up quietly in the night and opened all her gifts by herself. Needless to say, Christmas morning wasn't very exciting!

Another memory of the 5-1/2 years we spent in that house was the mice. They absolutely overran the place! The worst experience was the day I opened the tea towel drawer and one jumped out at me! I had trouble opening that drawer for a long while. One poor little creature jumped into an enclosure at the back of the stove that he could not exit from so he curled up and died. As time went along, every time we got close to the stove we could smell something dreadful. Finally Keith recovered the remains of that unfortunate little creature. The basement of the house had dirt floors and you entered it by lifting up a door that was in the floor. I won't forget the day that door was open when a young woman from the church came by with her 2-year old daughter. The child had just had a cast removed from a broken arm when she, unnoticed, found her way to the basement cavity and promptly fell down the stairs! Fortunately, because the floor was dirt and not cement, she didn't break any bones this time.

The Roblin church people treated us well. Our salary was actually considerably higher when we got there than it had been when we left Weyburn even though the congregation was less than half the size. They were a dedicated group. They finally decided that we needed a bigger house so a new parsonage was purchased in the residential area of the town. The price was $16,000. We often wished we had been in a position to purchase it ourselves because prices certainly escalated after 1973. That house was like a dream come true. It was a bungalow with a good-sized kitchen which included an eating area in the corner, a big living room, three bedrooms and a regular-sized bathroom on the main floor. The basement contained a small bedroom where Cameron slept, a bathroom, rec room, storage space and an open area which Keith turned into a shop.

One of the earlier family pictures in Roblin – in our purple and green coordinated outfits!

Marilou, as she got a little older and began to ride her tricycle around the neighbourhood, made friends with a couple she called Grandma and Grandpa Nolan. They treated her like a little princess. However, in time, Grandpa N. became a little too friendly and she didn't want to go there anymore. I feel badly that I was so naïve and, at first, couldn't see why - they seemed like such nice people. Grandpa would send her fancy valentine candies in the mail because he didn't want Grandma to know, which should have been a red flag. The sad ending to that story is that after her husband died, Grandma N., in her eighties, had a very frightening experience when she opened her home to a young man who knocked on her door. Tragically, he ended up raping her. She never recovered from the trauma.

When we arrived in Roblin, Cameron, who was in Grade three, attended a Primary school and Beth, in Grade four, an intermediate school which burned down that year. She completed her year in the town hall before the completion of the new Intermediate school for grades K-8. It was across the road from us and I never tired of the view out my kitchen window where I could watch the children playing in the schoolyard.

I spent a lot of hours in the schools there, subbing in every grade for most of the time we were there. One of my most pleasant experiences was a four-week stint of teaching Grade 10 literature to a group of very bright, eager students. One of the poems we studied was "My Love Is Like a Red, Red Rose." In my desire to convey what it was like to be in love, I went a little overboard and the students were amused by my feeble attempts to enlighten them. For weeks after that experience, I would meet those pupils on the main street of the town and they would look at me wistfully and recite, "My Love is like a Red, Red Rose."

I have had a life-long love of literature. I'm so glad that we memorized good poems in my school days. To this day I can quote Shakespeare's "The quality of mercy is not strained…" and that poignant poem "Abou Ben Adam." I have often quoted the line from that poem when observing a person who inspires me, "May his tribe increase." I have never forgotten the lines in Robert Frost's poem, "The Death of the Hired Man." How sad when your life experience is summed up in the lines, "Nothing to look backward to with pride and nothing to look forward to with hope."

Another enjoyable experience was teaching Home Economics for a teacher who was on maternity leave. One of the students from that class who stands out in my mind was a young Indian girl whose last name was Rattlesnake. She got teased mercilessly as people hissed when she walked by. I tried to give her special attention and at the end of the year she presented me with a pillow she had sewn. I treasured that gift.

One of the annual family involvements during our years in Roblin was participation in the Music Festivals. All of the kids were musical. Beth began taking piano lessons in Weyburn, where she had her first festival experience, performing in piano and voice at the age of eight. Cam and Marilou both started taking piano in Roblin. Marilou, at about the age of four joined a group class in which she learned the basics and had fun doing it. The children all played piano solos and duets, as well as singing. They were part of school choirs with excellent directors at the primary and secondary levels. We had many nail-biting experiences during fierce competitions. Sometimes the kids received trophies for their performances; sometimes they received a participation certificate. But it was a good learning experience. I spent many hours preparing a myriad of young people to sing in the festival, often accompanying them on the piano. One memory that stands out was the year in which Cameron, about 15 at the time, sang several times, capturing the heart of the adjudicator who provided a trophy just for him.

The last year or two at Roblin I became a piano teacher myself - mostly because there weren't enough teachers, not because I really felt qualified. One thing I remembered that my friend Doreen had told me was that I knew more than they did, which I guess was true. I had 17 students one year. It was an experience that was both frustrating and rewarding.

The children and I did lots of singing in those years. When Beth and Cameron were about 6 and 8 they began singing together. Our Conference Superintendent arranged for a pastoral exchange in which we spent a week in Prince Albert, Keith preaching each night and the children providing the special music. One of the memories of our singing experiences in Roblin included being on a TV variety show in Yorkton, Saskatchewan, about 50 miles away. Beth sang "The Teddy Bear's Picnic" and I sang, "He." One of the fun things that we did in Roblin was present children's musicals. One particular one, "His Fleece was White as Snow," was a memorable experience. I can still remember Mr. Rooster crowing to welcome the day and Snowy, the Lamb, who was chosen as the Passover sacrifice, realizing that he had to die. Other farm animals were involved in telling the story of Easter and the Risen Christ. The kids did an amazing job; some of those with leading roles had never sung a solo in their lives! Dave Church was the one behind the creation of the costumes and props that helped to make the musical such a success. It was our first experience of singing with a sound track.

One unforgettable day for me was when Cameron cut off half his thumb in the table saw. It was a school holiday and he was in the basement with a friend, cutting a board. I was on the phone when he appeared with a terrified look in his eyes. These words, "Look, Mom, my thumb" struck terror to my heart. I dropped the phone and called Keith, who was having a nap on the chesterfield. When they reached the hospital, they called to see if I could find the thumb, which I couldn't and wasn't sure I wanted to. In the end the Dr. thought it best to stitch it up since if it had been reattached it could have had no feeling. Though it was very upsetting at the time, it was amazing how little he suffered with it. He was able to do most things and even resumed piano lessons about a year later.

My teaching experiences were not all successful. Although I had always wanted to teach, I did not have that inexplicable magic touch that allowed me to be in complete control of the classroom at all times. From the time I did my practice teaching in Seattle, there seemed to always be one child that remained a challenge. The one full year that I taught Grade two was frustrating because I didn't start the year intending to teach full-time. I had many other commitments in my life at the time. I was called to teach on the second day of school in the fall. The teacher was coming back at Thanksgiving, then Christmas, but she ended up dying with cancer in February so, of course, I completed the year. The class was challenging because it was the top and the bottom of the Grade twos, a very distinct division and the teacher who was to teach them was one with a lot of experience so could have handled the situation so much better.

Marilou was in kindergarten that year and she was happy when I was teaching because she could play with the janitor's daughter while I was busy in my classroom, preparing for the next day. But Beth, who was in high school, preferred to have me home after school since she always unloaded her day's events on my waiting ear. When I was offered the job the second year I turned it down because I felt I couldn't handle full-time teaching while supporting my pastor husband, and being a good mother. Sometimes I have envied the ladies who were able to manage a teaching career along with other things, especially the pension they received at the end. But I never regretted that I was a mostly stay-at-home mom. I invested my time and energies mainly in our children and our church.

One day of substitute teaching was particularly bad. I was in a Grade eight classroom (never my favourite grade) where Cameron was in the class, something I didn't particularly like. It was a Math class and I had given the class an assignment. It was a Friday afternoon and the students became restless and began to get very unruly. I tried, unsuccessfully, to get them to work quietly. I had a toothache like I'd never had before and it began to get to me, along with the noise in the classroom. I sat at the desk with my head bowed so no one could see and I began to cry. I was embarrassed, especially for my son, but the pain was almost unbearable. I was soon saved by the bell and the kids filed out. Some of them glanced my way and I know there were some who regretted their actions. I felt quite gratified that the worst of the troublemakers came back after everyone was gone and apologized for his behaviour. I was in that same classroom after that on more than one occasion and they never gave me trouble again.

All the time we were in Roblin, we were part of the Shell River Bible Camp which was run mainly by members of our congregation. It was a children's camp in the daytime with a meeting for everyone, with a guest speaker, in the evening. We had some good times but sometimes it felt like a burden to be involved in two camps because every summer we attended Arlington Beach family camp which was always preceded by the annual conference, mandatory for all the pastors.

Beth and Cam performing at our 25th anniversary

One of the happy events that occurred in Roblin was the celebration of our 25th wedding anniversary in 1980. The congregation rented the Bield Hall and made it an unforgettable experience for us. Beth and Cam were both attending Aldersgate College at the time so they came home with friends and provided great music for the occasion, along with a humorous skit. Marilou was also part of the music. We were presented with a lovely silver casserole dish which contained 200 silver dollars! I could hardly believe the generosity of our congregation. The Taylor family organized another 25th anniversary celebration in the Wawota area which was attended by family and also friends who came from Weyburn. We felt richly blessed to have been honoured in such a gracious way.

The family on the occasion of our 25th anniversary celebration

During our tenure in Roblin, another significant event occurred, when we took a memorable trip to Seattle where we attended a Ministers' and wives conference. It was in the 70s when the Asbury Revival had spread to many places and some of the pastors had been touched by it. Revival has been described as "the Holy Spirit pointing his finger at you." And many of us experienced that. The sharing times with the pastors wives that I attended when the women became transparently honest were revealing and life-changing. Most of us began to deal with stuff that was unlike Christ—bad attitudes, bitterness toward people who we felt had hurt us and other sinful behaviours. After confession of sin in my life, I had a great sense of forgiveness and felt a new love for people that I hadn't felt for a long time. I went back to the church changed. As a result of that, there were things I had to make right—one of them being my attitude toward Shirley's husband, Alan. I wrote him a letter confessing my ill feelings toward him. I knew that it was no secret how I felt about him—I had made it quite clear that he wasn't my favourite person. I was elated when he phoned me in response and I'll never forget his words—"thanks for your letter and I love you for it." What a wonderful liberation from the bitterness I'd allowed to build for years. I was free! Since that time Alan and I have had a good relationship.

There were many confessions made and things made right those days as the Holy Spirit began to move among our people in Roblin as well. We held a series of inter-church meetings in the United Church where people from the two churches who had felt bitterness toward each other following the split in 1968 made peace with each other. It was wonderful as people began to forgive each other and be reconciled. The Sutera twins who were a big part of that revival movement were active in a preaching ministry over the next few years. Even in Melfort we saw some of the influences of that revival in our congregation.

Chapter 21:

What Started Sadly, Ended Well

Although we had arrived at the Roblin church with great reluctance, it proved to be the right place for us. God gave me a personal verse that encouraged me as we began to serve there. It was 2 Corinthians 9:8: "And God is able to make all grace abound to you, so that in all things at all times, having all that you need, you will abound in every good work." The superlatives in that verse are amazing! What was so disappointing to us initially became 13 years of our most productive ministry. The first years were maintenance years when we endeavoured to encourage the dispirited group that was left after the split. In that body of believers, we discovered some of the most sincere, committed people we had ever met.

Our family when Beth and Cam were getting ready to leave the nest!

One of the biggest encouragements in Roblin was an outreach to a community of mostly relatives who were completely unchurched. There were about 10 of them who committed their lives to Christ and it was sheer joy to watch them grow. We had evening sessions in their homes where we answered their questions and taught them hymns and gospel songs. They were excited but not more than we were. We saw the church grow from about 40 when we arrived to 100.

We were pleased with the school system in Roblin and felt that our kids received a good education. I had a little difficulty with the fact that the principal of the Intermediate School was an alcoholic and often missed days of school. On one occasion there was a teachers' in-service on alcoholism but the principal was home sick. When he would come to my desk first thing in the morning, the smell of alcohol was strong on his breath. But the powers that be overlooked it and he continued to keep his job until retirement. But most of the teachers were the kind the children respected. I will always remember when Cam (by this time he wasn't called Cameron any more) was in Grade 11 and was given a book to read which contained very coarse language, including lots of use of the "f" word. Without any input from us, Cam decided the book wasn't fit to read so he reported that decision to his English teacher. As a result, he was given the opportunity to choose another book and report on it. We were proud of him. He had a very tender conscience and was appalled that Beth had gone with her friends to see the movie, *One Flew Over the Cookoo`s Nest*. He had simply heard the kids talking about it at school and concluded that it wasn`t something a Christian should watch.

Cam was a very self-disciplined kid and always did his work without complaining. When his dad asked him to mow the lawn, it was done. When he was taking piano lessons, he would be up early and the first thing I heard in the morning was the sound of him practicing in the basement where he slept. For some reason, we were storing a piano for someone, I don't even know who. There was one place where Cam could have been accused of procrastination and that was his school assignments, like essays. They were always finished the night before they were due and who was the person to make that happen? Me. My typing skills came in handy. It meant translating his handwriting which was almost indecipherable.

Another teacher, Wayne Densmore, became a special friend of Beth's when he was her homeroom teacher in Grade seven. He was a dedicated teacher and friend of all the kids. He had lots of modern technology in his room - played the kids' kind of music and had them create videos. He never went to the staff room at noon hour. He was a perfect mix of caring and strictness, creating a good learning environment. He also taught Cameron and Marilou as they came along. Later Wayne and his wife, Carol, became friends of ours because of the kids. They didn't attend our church but were loyal friends. They helped us move to Melfort, then Eyebrow, and finally Moose Jaw. Unfortunately, Wayne wasn't well enough to be there for the move to Weyburn. He struggled with his health, was asthmatic among other things, and died in 2002. He was just 63. But we have maintained a friendship with his widow ever since, a wonderful caring woman.

When Beth was 15 she went to work for the summer, babysitting for a farm family who lived half-an-hour away. She had some interesting experiences. On one occasion the family went camping and left the baby home with Beth and her friend Diane who was a niece of the mother's. The baby developed diarrhea which was quite traumatic. They ended up washing clothes but had a disaster when somehow water ended up all over the floor. She phoned home in great distress. When I think of the two girls alone with a baby at a farm with no transportation, even if they had been able to drive, I shudder at the thought. But she survived and gained a valuable experience.

Another learning experience for Beth was the summer she rode the bus to Red Deer, Alberta where she helped my friend, Doreen after the birth of her twin girls. There were also three boys in the family. It was quite a summer! I remember one letter when Beth said that she was getting used to the yelling and screaming for it was quite a chaotic household. Doreen was never a fussy housekeeper so Beth, the particular one, had her work cut out for her cleaning the house and helping care for the children.

Beth was always very involved at school. She loved participating in drama and choir, sometimes as the pianist. There were times that I felt she was too involved, to the neglect of her studies and her piano practicing. She had to drive thirty miles to take her piano lessons. When she was preparing for her Grade nine exam, which was to be in Regina, she was just not practicing as I felt she should. I went into her room one night and reminded her in no uncertain terms that this was costing us money and she was going to fail her exam if she didn't smarten up! However, her dad was praying diligently that she would pass - which amazingly, she did. Later I had to eat humble pie and apologize for the way I had spoken to her. What I said was right but not the way I said it.

One of the things that caused some distraction for Beth was her first boyfriend, Chuck. There were no Christian guys in Roblin so we allowed her to date Chuck, who came from a good home. I went to a ladies retreat where in the washroom the topic of our teenagers and dating came up. I said that we allowed Beth to date a non-Christian. The response that I got from one of the ladies was vehement. In no uncertain terms she informed me that I should never allow that to happen. Another guy Beth dated later was a nice guy with a sweet personality. He was her graduation escort and he was crazy about her but she broke up with him because he wasn't a Christian. She was a girl with strong convictions.

When Beth was going into Grade 12 she decided she wanted to be student body president of her school, Goose Lake High. She was diligent in the task. At her graduation in 1977 we were so proud of her. Tears came to my eyes as she walked down the aisle in her beautiful yellow dress as the grads entered the gym. In introducing her at the grad exercises, the principal said, "Precious things come in small packages," referring to her height. She was only five feet tall.

Cam was not quite as involved as Beth but he nevertheless, made his mark. In his last year he had the rather mundane task of filling the Coke machine, which he did faithfully. One of his interests was ping pong, a game in which he did very well. He had a good friend who often came to our house to practice. He also participated in track and field where he excelled as a sprinter. It was a joy to see him compete. It proved to be a forerunner to his interest in running marathons, which he did many times. One of his dreams was to compete in the Boston marathon but that never became a reality.

Another of Cam's interests was hockey. That started when we lived in Weyburn when he was very young. From his earliest experiences on the ice he clamored to be the goalie which was his position as long as he played hockey. I can say that the only time I was truly a hockey fan was when Cam played. When he was about 14, for various reasons, he chose not to play anymore. We had some conflicts with the sport because he was expected to play on Sunday and we held to Sunday being observed as a special day. We felt that young kids shouldn't have to choose between hockey and Sunday School. The team didn't like it when he wasn't there because he was the best goalie. It was hard for me to see him hurt over what was our decision. We did let him go to Flin Flon with the team for a tournament because we felt he would never have the opportunity to see that northern Manitoba town again.

One of Cam's achievements in Roblin when he was about 15 was to buy and restore a car that had been damaged in an accident. He and his friend, Dave from Macleods store spent hours together pounding out the dints and turning that forest green vehicle into a thing of beauty. It served him well for many years after. Dave and Cam had lots of shared experiences since Dave had hired Cam to put bikes together at the store about the same year. As soon as he had his driver's license, Dave allowed him to drive his much treasured truck, a privilege not awarded to many.

When Cam graduated from high school we were very proud when, to our surprise, he received the Staff Award. The recipient was chosen by the teachers to be given to an all-round good student, who had contributed to school life, had been active in sports, while doing well in his studies. Even filling the Coke machine didn't go unnoticed!

I did quite a variety of things in the 13 years we lived in Roblin. In addition to the substitute teaching I did, I was director of the CYC (Christian Youth Crusaders), led the children's choir, prepared cantatas with an adult choir, was president of the Music Festival Association, and sang in the community choir. I also belonged to a Pro-Life group. After a speech I had given on the subject, I was invited to give the homily at a Catholic church in the area at their Saturday evening service.

One of my favourite things about living in the parsonage was the opportunities I had to practice the gift of hospitality. I have always enjoyed cooking and baking and had many opportunities to share my gifts with a variety of different guests. We entertained, not only our parishioners and occasionally family members, but also visiting missionaries, evangelists, church leaders, and even bishops. I felt that the lives of our children were enriched by the presence of these godly people in our home. I believe that when we give, we receive.

The most fulfilling experience I had was starting the Friendship Bible Coffee ministry in the area. An evangelical girl hosted it (a member of the church that had split from ours), a committed Catholic girl attended and I led the first study. It grew until we had several groups and we also had an annual Friendship Bible Coffee banquet. I was one of the leaders until the coordinator came to me to say that I shouldn't be doing it because I was a pastor's wife. At that time our group contained Catholics, Ukrainian Orthodox, United Church and one Evangelical woman who didn't seem to be bothered about what denomination I belonged to. They thought that I was better trained to lead it than anybody. Though I was deeply disappointed and wrote a letter of protest to Stonecroft, the sponsor of the studies, I dropped out for a while but when they couldn't get anyone else, I was allowed to break the rules and step back in.

It was wonderful to see the girls growing in their faith, some of them learning to pray for the first time. I invited one of my neighbours who had been raised Catholic and had taken her schooling in a convent, but wasn't attending church. She had a small son (their only birth son after three adopted children) who wasn't in school so Keith agreed to babysit him to enable her to attend. She was quite protective of him but did trust him to Keith. She became a believer through that first study, the Gospel of Mark.

One year when the Grandview church (a town east of Roblin) was left without a resident pastor, I became a temporary "preacher." Because both congregations wanted an eleven-o'clock service, Keith and I alternated between the towns so that I only had to prepare a sermon every two weeks. I've always enjoyed speaking so did not consider it a burden. I have had other opportunities to speak over the years, particularly at ladies meetings.

One of the traumatic experiences for me in Roblin was a miscarriage. I will never forget the day. I was subbing in a Grade one class when I began having cramps. Because I was 37 at the time, I probably should have seen a doctor but I was too busy to bother. It was most disappointing because it was to be the fourth child we'd always wanted and in addition to that, a little playmate for Marilou who was so much younger than her siblings. It happened in the middle of the night. Dr. Jones, our wonderful lady doctor came to the house when Keith called her to say that I was bleeding profusely (it was considered a "late abortion" since I was three-and-one-half months along). The next day I was lying in the hospital bed on intravenous when two young women from the church came in with a dozen yellow roses. I burst into tears. Another thing that had brought tears to my eyes was the unsympathetic words of the nurse's aide who scolded me for crying with the words, "Tears don't help anything." How wrong she was. My understanding of tears is that they are therapeutic.

Another memory that I have often shared over the years was an experience I had while on a plane trip to see Mom and Dad in B.C. Beth and Marilou were with me and we were travelling with an older lady who was also planning to visit family in B.C. I had gotten off the plane in Edmonton to phone my friend, Doreen. Because the Klondike Days were on, there was a great deal of noise and confusion with people singing and milling about in period costumes in the area where I was phoning. I plugged my ears so I could hear and apparently missed the announcement that it was time for me to board my plane for my flight to Regina. When I was making my way back to the plane after what I thought was the right amount of time, I heard the call, "Would Joan Taylor please report to Gate-such-and-such." I began to run and when I reached the gate, the plane was nowhere to be seen. It had taken off down the runway without me. Marilou was about a year old and Beth 11. The lady travelling with us informed the stewardess that the mother of these children was not on the plane. She dropped her magazines and hurried to the cockpit where she announced the problem. Then, surprisingly, I saw the plane turn around and head back. They brought back the stairs and I climbed up them, happy to be reunited with my children! Someone said to me, "You must feel pretty important!" Actually the feeling was more embarrassment! Keith would have been very upset if the children had arrived at the airport in Regina without me on board.

Chapter 22:

Some of the Not-so-Happy Experiences in the Parsonage

I can't write an autobiography without making reference to the difficult times that we experienced in the churches we served, because that is part of living. I can't say that I looked at trials biblically, "counting them all joy," but I know that they are valuable teachers just the same. Sometimes I felt very lonely and isolated from family, especially on special occasions like Christmas and New Year's. One year we had planned to go to Taylors for New Year's but a gentleman from the church died and the funeral was to be the day after the holiday. They even brought in a former pastor to officiate but we had to be present. We were alone on that special day without having made any special food preparations. Woefully, all I could think of was that people were celebrating with family and we were alone.

There were conflicts in the church that were hurtful. Legalism was entrenched in the thinking of some of the people in Roblin but, for the most part, we were able to see beyond that to their heart. While, in our opinion, they had made mistakes in judgment in some instances, their desire was to serve God to the best of their ability.

I cannot deny that some of the legalism was hurtful. Keith got into hassles more than once when he referred to any version of the Bible other than the King James Version. At one point in a church meeting, one of the older men turned in his Sunday School quarterly because it had some Scripture printed in it that was not from the KJV. His explanation was, "I won't have this in my house!" Keith tried to explain that the KJV was just a translation like the newer ones and that the original languages of the Bible were Hebrew and Greek. The offended party had never heard of such a thing. His response was, "Are you sure?" We realized then that their prejudices were based on ignorance more than anything. But the strong opinions never altered. Keith always read from the KJV from the pulpit which kept the criticism to a minimum. He would use other translations but only to make an explanation, never to identify it. To say that the New International Version (NIV) or other translations are more accurate than the KJV would have been pure heresy!

One of my favourite ages to teach was the Young Adults, which I did for most of the time we were in Roblin. They were teachable and we had great discussions. The problem with many of the older adults is that they had a concrete mindset. This surfaced when I was teaching the adult Sunday School class on one occasion. I felt hurt when one of the gentlemen disagreed with something I had said and reported to his grandchildren that I was not teaching the Bible. The kids came from a non-Christian home and their grandpa brought them to Sunday School each week. In fact, of his five children and his wife, no one was a believer. His church attendance under Keith's ministry came to an abrupt end on a Sunday when a visiting group of young people, The Heatherington Singers, came to our church and presented a concert at the opening of Sunday School.

It was in the 70's when the girls wore miniskirts. Keith kind of gulped when he saw them but never thought of turning them away when they arrived because of how they were dressed. Furthermore, at the conclusion of their songs he thanked them for coming and said we had enjoyed their presentation. He was met at the door by some very irate parishioners, one of whom made a comment that he would have met them at the door with a whip. In response Keith asked the question, "Could you have done that in love?" He replied that he guessed not. Another man walked out after Sunday School and never came back to hear Keith preach again! In this man's mind, Keith had committed the unpardonable sin. Most of the people, however, were willing to chalk it up to what they considered as a mistake in judgment. It took time but most of the distressed ones forgave their pastor.

It was a difficult experience for me when one couple threatened to leave the church when I thanked another couple publically at the end of the annual Christmas program. Those were always big events and most years I was in charge. We endeavoured to have "all-church" presentations so we would have more than 50 people to the practices. Some of the children were rambunctious and practices weren't always fun. This particular year a young man, Dave Church, offered to give leadership to the practices. He had been a teacher and had come to town with his brother to manage a hardware store which they had purchased. It was such a gift to me that I wanted to acknowledge it. I thanked him and his wife, who played the piano and attended every practice, and presented them with a box of chocolates. The offended couple told my husband that I was showing favouritism, likening it to Joseph's coat of many colours. Eventually they forgave me for my insensitivity and never did leave the church, even though we did not see them for some time. However, as a result, I learned to reward people more privately.

I led a group of the young teens that was sometimes very challenging. They came to our house, not by choice, while their parents went to the church for the weekly prayer meeting. We had some good discussions but they were never an open group. None of them really made a commitment to the Lord, in spite of the many years they attended church and summer Bible camp. I have two not very positive memories of those Young Teen gatherings. One was a time when they came to our house on a Wednesday night and were waiting downstairs for me to begin the study. I noticed that a big bottle of Coke was missing from the bathroom (which was also storage). No one would confess to taking it and I never found out who took it. I always felt badly that someone would not only take it, but also deny it.

Another time we had planned an overnight camping experience at Madge Lake, a beautiful place not far away. We had planned together what we would eat and what we would do and everyone seemed to be excited about the plan. The only demand I made of them was that they tell me if they were going to leave the campsite. We got to the park and one of the guys was already missing, without saying one word. After looking all over for him, he finally showed up. That was frustrating. But then I went to say Goodnight to the girls in their tent when I spied a pack of cigarettes sitting on the bed. Of course, no one would own up to that either. As you might expect, it was my one and only time that I took a group of Young Teens camping!

The heartwarming end of that story is that the main troublemaker in that group (the one who wandered off without telling) later became a devoted follower of Christ. He was one of three sons who came from a family where the mother was a committed Christian and the father an alcoholic. The middle brother was a Christian and the younger brother later came to Christ as well. It was such a feel-good moment a number of years later to receive a letter from this young man to say thank you for the years we had taught him biblical truths. He always was a likeable kid – just full of mischief. It's a miracle he's still alive. On one occasion he raced across the road to beat a car and was hit by it, sending him to hospital and into traction for some time. Another summer he fell while swinging and broke an arm. Because he couldn't do much at home, his mother sent him to another summer camp. With one arm in a cast, he was fooling around on the teeter totter when he fell and broke the other one. Later as a young adult, having had a little too much to drink, he fell several stories and landed on his feet, injured but alive. His life is a testament of God's grace and mercy.

Their alcoholic dad was such a nice guy but on weekends he usually went on drinking binges. Sometimes he would show up drunk at Christmas programs which would be embarrassing for his boys. We have been to their house when he was passed out at the kitchen table. On one occasion, he called us to go to their home because his wife, Ada, couldn`t speak. She had been so traumatized by a near accident that she couldn`t utter an intelligent word. He had gotten into the car drunk. She wanted to drive but he wouldn`t let her and belligerently took the wheel. He saw a car coming but decided to pass anyway and she was sure they were going to crash. They survived but she was in shock from the incident and had to go to the hospital for treatment. She was a wonderful woman. In the end her husband also came to faith in Christ before he died.

We had some traumatic experiences in Roblin. The first one, not long after we arrived, was a drowning death of a 27-year-old man who stepped into the Shell River on a hot Sunday afternoon and never came up. He left a wife and three young boys. The oldest, Chester, about six years old at the time watched as they pulled his dad's body from the river. Keith had been called to the scene and had the horrible responsibility of informing his mom and dad. A devastating time for all the family.

Another sad day was when we were on vacation and received a call that little two-and-a-half-year-old, Melora had been hurt on a swing at her family farm. Her dad had made the swing and her sister, Melissa, was pushing her when it tipped over and hit her, fatally wounding her. We went to the funeral chapel with the family the day before the funeral where the mother balked at every step. The doll they had put in Melora's arms refused to stay in place, a memory that haunts me. That was probably the saddest funeral of all. Melora was so full of life. Keith, who called her "Smiley," felt that he needed all the experience he'd had to officiate that day. It was also difficult for the teenaged girls who sang the song, "Through It All."

A discouraging thing that we had to deal with in different congregations was animosity between members. In ladies Bible studies, I stressed the importance of following the clear guidelines for healthy relationships from Colossians 3:12-14: "Therefore, as God's chosen people, holy and dearly loved, clothe yourselves with compassion, kindness, humility, gentleness and patience. Bear with each other and forgive whatever grievances you may have against one another. Forgive as the Lord forgave you. And over all these virtues put on love…" Love--always the key.

Another disappointing thing that we experienced was seeing marriages disintegrate. We always considered our church people "family" and it's hard to see the family hurting, because in the loss of a marriage many people are affected. When we saw our young people lose interest in the church, it was also difficult.

Basically our years in Roblin were good ones. We left many friends behind. Our children called some of the older people "Aunt" and "Uncle" and they treated them like family. We started up a group called "Pairs and Spares" (not very politically correct) which provided us with lots of social events where we did everything from horseback riding to tobogganing (my last ride left me with severe tendonitis that took many months to heal - reminding us that we weren't as young as we once were). But it was fun. We had many wonderful meals in the homes of some of the parishioners. They loved to play games so times in their homes almost always included one game or another.

After thirteen years in Roblin, we felt that it was time for us to move on, that perhaps someone new would be good for the church, so we asked for a new appointment. By this time things had progressed to the point where the conference superintendent would give you two or three options and you could go to the one that was most appealing. Melfort was one of the churches that was open at the time so it was back to Saskatchewan for us.

Chapter 23:

The Melfort Church Community

The Melfort church was located in a very prosperous farming community. We enjoyed driving through the countryside where trees lined the roads, the land was rich and productive, and farmsteads were picture perfect. It was close to the pines, unlike the southern part of the province. We did some cross-country skiing through the pines where you were protected from the winds. We didn't find that sport very satisfactory in the flat, windy prairie where we lived after we left Melfort. The church was an attractive, brick structure with laminated beams. It looked like a church! We lived about half a block away which was very handy.

The Melfort Free Methodist Church

Marilou, who was in Grade eight when we moved there, soon found friends and made a good adjustment. In grades eight and nine she took part in the Credit Union public speaking contest, speaking on the subjects of Abortion and Marijuana, placing first both times. There were several teenagers her age in the church so her social life was pretty full. I loved having the kids hang out at our house and was able to feel connected during those five years.

Substitute teaching in the schools there wasn't a possibility for me so I took a job as accompanist for the choirs in Grades 9-12. I enjoyed working with the director, Tim Huebert, who was such an encouragement. I would have given up much sooner if he hadn't kept telling me I could do it. I don't think I've ever practiced more on the piano. Some of the pieces were beyond me but I struggled to master them. Off-beat rhythms were never my forte. I also worked part-time in the school office where I had my first experience with computers. It was an Apple and although I was a little frightened of it, I was fascinated by what it could do. The office staff, including the principal and my co-workers, were great to work with. I was in the staff room the day the Challenger blew up – that was a moment to remember since a teacher was on that flight and the last memory of her was that smiling, happy person who was waving to everyone before she entered the cockpit.

Another thing I remember about my school experience there was giving an announcement over the intercom that someone should come to the foy**er**. Quickly Marilou and her friends appeared to tell me that it was not pronounced foy**er** but foy**ay**. How our children do teach us! I enjoyed the young people during those years, both in class and whenever we went on choir trips. They fondly called me Mrs. T.

Marilou always had a passion for music. She had an excellent piano teacher in Melfort who made her work very hard. She hosted monthly recitals and had high expectations for her students. Marilou took part in music festivals, both singing and playing piano and did well. Music also played a big part in her life in high school as she was in the jazz ensemble, the band and choirs. She was delighted to land the part of Mrs. Bumble in *Oliver*, a musical that the school performed. As a member of the Jazz Band she attended Expo 86 in Vancouver, a great experience. I was president of the Music Parents Association for a time which was interesting. I well remember the time we collected garbage on the highway as a fundraiser when we had about six people turn up to work. I recall grumbling with a Mormon woman and her son as we picked up cigarette cartons and beer cans, something neither of us would be discarding, along with other pieces of refuse. Somehow it didn't seem fair that six of us were slaving for the benefit of the whole group. But who says life is fair?

Marilou's high school graduation was a memorable event. She looked lovely in a pink dress which had been a bridesmaid dress worn by Vicky. I always appreciated the fact that Marilou didn't demand a new, expensive dress for graduation. Small town graduations are special events. There was a mothers and grads tea which was most enjoyable. The graduation exercises and dance took place in the evening. I was privileged to give a speech on behalf of the parents of the grads - a proud moment for me. The Christian young people had a party that evening but Marilou could not stay up all night as some of her friends did. She had to be in Saskatoon to take her Grade 10 piano exam the next day! She had suffered with dermatitis in her hands for years. They had broken out just in time for her exam and in playing her pieces she left drops of blood all over the piano keys. It was a stressful time and we were worried that she might not be successful in her exam. But she passed - a great victory!

One of the memorable experiences in Melfort was the addition of a beautiful cat to our family. We had had cats before and they were always welcome in our home. More than once our children prayed for the cats when they disappeared but they always came back. However, we had a neighbour in Roblin who hated our cat with a passion. Unfortunately, he invaded her flower garden which wasn't acceptable. One day, through her husband, she came with an ultimatum - either you get rid of your cat or we will! To Marilou's great disappointment we couldn't keep him, so found a farm family willing to take him. That cat story ended rather sadly.

Now we were faced with another cat-decision. Marilou's friend came to me when I was in the school office one fall day and asked if she could give Marilou a kitten for Christmas. We reluctantly consented, knowing how much our daughter loved animals. We named her Whiskers because that was what defined her. She turned out to be a wonderful pet that we all became very attached to. Keith made her a little house to shelter her if she came back home when we were away. One night when we arrived, we found her in her house, obviously in pain. She had evidently been badly injured so Keith and Marilou took her to the vet. The word was that she had a broken hip and needed surgery to repair it. When they called me about the surgery I responded, "It's only a cat." However, this did not sit well with either Marilou or her dad so I gave my consent to the surgery. They put in a pin and the cost was $127. I could hardly believe that Keith was willing to spend the money but she was well worth the cost.

Life in the Melfort Church had its ups and downs. There were several couples about our age and we had many good times in their homes. They took us into their hearts and twice we were invited to someone's home for Christmas when we were unable to be with family (particularly when Christmas fell on a Sunday). Some of the best meals we've ever eaten were served by wonderful cooks in that church community. We worked hard in the church, trying to keep up a full program but many of our efforts were unsuccessful. It seemed like all the Christian families who came to town ended up at the Covenant Church which was flourishing. One experience was particularly disappointing when a couple left our church, placing a note under the door of the study. It would have been nice if they had been able to talk to us!

We had an older person in our church (the one who had been my first piano teacher in Cadillac) who made my life difficult at times. She was very jealous of her position at the organ and thought she should ALWAYS play. She was getting deaf so wasn't able to keep in time with the piano which was located on the opposite side of the room. Consequently, the music was draggy, something which I found intolerable. So on an Easter Sunday she had arrived later than usual and I decided (not very wisely, I'll admit) to play the organ and have Marilou on the piano so that we could have lively music on that special Sunday. When she came in and saw me on the organ bench she was furious! How dare I take her spot! Standing beside my husband, I always greeted the congregation at the door after the service and that day when she came by she came as close to spitting in my face as anyone ever did. She wouldn't speak to me so finally I knew I had to go to her. She received me rather coldly and proceeded to tell me about all the times she had been ill-treated by people in the churches she had been part of. I admitted that what I had done was wrong. In conclusion I said to her, "But we can't become bitter over these things," to which she responded, "Oh, I'm not bitter." She could have fooled me! Going back with baggage from 40 years ago sounded to me like she had a problem. But after that experience she forgave me and was loyal to us. Keith led her husband to Christ after he had had a heart attack and she was very thankful for that. Keith officiated at the funerals of both of them quite a few years later.

Chapter 24:

Our Children's Weddings

Two happy events occurred while we were living in Melfort - the weddings of Beth and Cam. They both took place in the First Free Methodist Church in Moose Jaw. Beth has been living there since completing two years of biblical studies at Aldersgate College. She was employed as Dining Hall Hostess at the college as well as choir director and organist at the Minto United Church in that city. In the fall of 1981, a young man arrived at the college from Whitby, Ontario by the name of Barry Rawn. He had just recommitted his life to the Lord and was in limbo before he began an apprenticeship at General Motors in January. He was soon very much in love with a young woman from the prairies named Beth. Their first date was at the college fundraising dinner in September when Art Linkletter was the featured speaker. We were in attendance so met Barry that night. There was very little time in one short semester to get acquainted and Barry was much more interested in the young woman he'd met than his studies. He wanted to spend every possible moment with her, even bending the rules occasionally if necessary, because she was on staff at the college. Many a night she had to practically kick him out the door! By mid-December when the term was finished and he was leaving for home, he detoured by Melfort in the hopes of spending a little more time together. Their courtship was a stressful one, many hours of it spent on the phone getting to know one another.

In March Beth made a trip to Ontario, chauffeuring Nickie Stansberry, the dean of women and beautiful singer, who was doing a promotional tour. On that trip she and Barry were engaged. Obviously, Barry's mom and dad wondered about this girl their son was planning to marry for when they announced their engagement, Barry's mom burst into tears. No doubt she was in shock and perhaps disappointed that he hadn't chosen one of the many girls that the family knew who lived nearer home. Because the young couple wanted to spend every minute together, they arrived at the plane late for Beth's return flight. After explaining their circumstances, the soft-hearted attendant allowed Beth to transfer to another flight without charge. Barry returned to Saskatchewan in April to attend Cam's graduation from the Bachelor of Theology program. He met our family at that time for both sets of grandparents were in attendance also. That was when their engagement was officially announced.

Beth and Barry Rawn

The wedding took place August 28, 1982, not quite a year after they had met. It was a happy event with about 250 in attendance. Since my dad did the introductory part of the ceremony, Keith had the privilege of walking our eldest daughter down the aisle and then officiating at the ceremony which was beautiful. The music was heavenly - provided by musicians from the church playing violins and piano. Beth was a radiant bride. For Marilou, one of Beth`s attendants, it was not a happy day as she anticipated Beth`s upcoming move so far away (1700 miles away, to be exact). The guest list was very lopsided as only seven of the guests were from Ontario, which I'm sure must have been a disappointment to Barry`s family. Attending were Barry's mom and dad, sister Kristine and her husband Terry, Aunt Dorothy and best friends, Bob and Bonnie Snider. There were many speeches, some of them rather long, (like the sermon given by much-loved Grandpa Campbell) and a variety of musical items at the reception which was held in the college dining hall. Nickie Stansberry sang *In His Time,* a song that had special meaning for Beth as she was assured that God had someone for her in His time.

It became apparent that the hour was too late for the opening of the gifts that were piled high. For me, that was a big disappointment because I knew that it would be a long time before I would see those gifts. But there was no changing Barry's mind when the certainty of that fact was presented to me. Afterward I heard that Barry had declared that he won that round with his new mother-in-law!

There was a huge vacancy in our family life without Beth coming home any more for Christmas or special occasions. She had never lived farther than four hours away which made it possible for us to visit her whenever we felt the need. The adjustment for Beth was also huge as she was suddenly thrust into a totally new environment far from family, surrounded by strangers, including a husband she hardly knew. But the vows they made to each other at that ceremony symbolized a deep commitment. They have been a couple who have learned to communicate well. They celebrated their 30th anniversary in 2012.

Following his graduation from Aldersgate with his Bachelor of Theology degree, Cam lived with us in Melfort, before heading to Western Theological Seminary in Portland, Oregon in the fall. He worked hard painting that summer. It was a treat to have him home one more time before he would be embarking on his new life as a husband and a pastor.

Cam was married the following year on August 20, 1983 to Vicky Parkins whose mom and dad were on staff at Aldersgate College, Gene as Business Manager and Helen, as music teacher. We had first heard Helen play at Seattle Pacific College where she and Gene were students at the same time we were. Helen, an accomplished pianist and violinist, along with Vicky's brother John on the cello, were part of the beautiful chamber music provided at the wedding. It was a lovely ceremony in which Keith again had the privilege of officiating. We were pleased to have all of our family members on both sides in attendance.

Cam and Vicky (Parkins) Taylor

We had a roast beef rehearsal dinner in the church basement the night before which was attended by all the relatives who had come from a distance. It was a fun time. Cam and Vicky spent their first year of marriage at the seminary in Portland. An internship in the church in Moose Jaw completed Cam's final year of seminary studies. Their pastoral ministry extended to Red Deer, Alberta and finally to Abbotsford, B.C. where Cam pastored for 17 years. They were married 30 years in 2013.

Chapter 25:

A Whole New World – Grandparenting

Our first five precious grandchildren-
Shannon, Ryan, Justin, Caleb, Elena

.I have always considered parenting to be one of the most rewarding things I have done in my life. Being entrusted with the lives of children is a special privilege and I do value the hours I spent talking to them, helping them with their problems, rejoicing with them in their successes, suffering with them in their disappointments and encouraging them whenever it was needed. We are so grateful that all of them chose to follow Christ as young children. I have always said that I would have had great difficulty dealing with rebellious kids.

Beth's children—Shannon, Ryan and Justin

Then when you think your hands-on parenting has come to an end, another wonderful world opens up - grandparenting. On May 10th, 1985, Beth and Barry presented us with our first grandchild, Shannon

Elizabeth. She has been a delight to us her whole life. She was joined by a brother, Ryan Campbell, June 15, 1987 and Justin Kenneth June 12, 1990. The boys have been such great pals as they've grown up. We watched them grow from a distance and enjoyed their visits West every other year and our trips East. But it was hard to be an involved long-distance grandparent and sometimes I felt cheated when I saw grandparents attending church with their families and celebrating special occasions together. I often felt lonely and far away from our children and grandchildren.

When Shannon was 13 she flew out to visit us in Weyburn. An observant child, I found her fascinating. We both love baking; on one occasion we created cinnamon buns together. She still brings us samples of her delicious baking. One of her kitchen necessities was a large mixer that she has made much use of.

**Cam and Vicky's children—
Caleb and Elena**

Cam and Vicky's children did not arrive in the conventional way. In 1990 when Romanian orphanages were opening up to adoptions, Cam made a 4-week trip to that country, in search of a family to love. They found two beautiful children, Caleb Marius Ross, born September 17, 1989, and Elena Michelle born July 24, 1990. It was a stressful time, especially when Caleb's birth mother was being pressured not to give up Caleb since his dad had been killed. After much prayer at this end, Caleb was released to come. They arrived in Canada with their new dad November 7th, 1990. The trip was a challenge for Cam with a 3-month old baby and a 13-month old child. An eighty-year old lady was happy to assist him with the baby. Vicky home schooled the children until Elena was in Grade six and Caleb in Grade 8. They both have done well in school. They have brought a lot of joy to all of us.

Chapter 26:

Time for Change and Another Family Wedding

Marilou graduated from high school in 1986 and it seemed like a logical time for us to move on. She was planning to attend Bible College in Moose Jaw so when the church at Eyebrow was open, we accepted the challenge. Since Eyebrow was only 50 miles away and Moose Jaw was our business town, I knew we would be able to see our "baby girl" fairly frequently, something that seemed important when we were experiencing the "empty nest."

The Eyebrow Parsonage

Eyebrow was a small village of 206, according to the 1986 census. I had often travelled through small places and said to Keith, "Don't ever take me to a place this small." But here we were! It had some disadvantages, to be sure, but we found it to be a very friendly place where we soon got to know just about everyone in town.

At 51, I felt too young to join the "old folks" at the Seniors Centre, but I finally submitted. We enjoyed many pleasant hours there – sharing monthly dinners, playing games (Keith acquired his first real interest in pool) and getting to know the villagers. I directed a community choir during those years and we put on some excellent cantatas which were a joy to everyone. I played on a ladies curling team, was involved in the women`s ministry at the church and led a neighbourhood Bible study.

Although I did some subbing in the local schools, I felt the need for something more. When the job opportunity came up for a part-time secretary to the Conference Superintendent, Joe James, in Moose Jaw, I jumped at the idea. We soon got into a routine. It was a 45 minute trip so I left at 8:10, arriving at the office at 8:55. I was not home much before 6:00 so Keith prepared supper (if I left specific menu suggestions). I edited the newsletter, among other duties and found the work stimulating and fulfilling. In 1990 when Joe James assumed the role of president of Aldersgate College he invited me to be his secretary there.

Our lovely new home in Moose Jaw - our first

Keith had been feeling for some time the need to leave pastoral ministry and had occasionally talked about the maintenance position at Aldersgate, thinking he could still have some influence on the young men who were in ministerial training, while doing something less stressful. The position was open that year so we moved to Moose Jaw in the summer of 1990, into our new home on the campus. It was an enjoyable experience making decisions about carpets, flooring and decorating for it was the first home that was our own, after 32 years of living in church owned parsonages.

In the meantime, the story of our cat Whiskers continued. She had moved with us to Eyebrow and then to Moose Jaw which offered her many opportunities to hunt in the open areas which surrounded our new home. She followed Keith in his evening rounds of the campus, acting more like a dog than a cat. One summer when we had taken a trip to Ontario to visit Beth's family and were preparing to leave the following morning, we got a phone call from a girl who had been employed at the college. She informed us that she had something that belonged to us - our cat! She had hopped into Joanne's moving truck and ridden to Ontario where five days later they discovered her, safe and sound. She hated car-riding but we were able to get a sedative to keep her calm for the long return trip home. The sad ending of the story is that she was later lost forever when Marilou was looking after her and took her to a camping area in a rural area. She didn't want to go into the motorhome where they were staying. Marilou's last words to her were, "Whiskers, don't go away." She was never seen again. It was a great loss, especially to Keith who grieved deeply. He even put a "lost cat" ad in the paper with her picture. We also visited farms in the area where she had been last seen—to no avail.

Our favourite family pet--Whiskers

Marilou had done a variety of things since her first year at Aldersgate. She had lived in Saskatoon in her own apartment for a while, working in a nursing home while she completed her ARCT in piano. She was able to buy a piano because of the generosity of a resident at the Melfort nursing home where she had been employed the summer after graduation. Then she returned to Aldersgate for one more year. After completing that year she continued to live in Moose Jaw where she became a resident attendant at St. Anthony's Nursing Home. Although living at home was convenient and less expensive, we understood her need for independence when she moved into her own apartment with a girl who was employed by the college. It was a comfort to know she was just across the back alley from us. She still enjoyed some of the privileges of home, like free laundry service.

In 1992 Marilou became engaged to Jay Mowchenko, a young ministerial student from Moose Jaw, and they were married July 24, 1993. It was a lovely wedding – Marilou a beautiful bride. It was another family affair with Beth and Cam's boys as ring bearers, Shannon as candle-lighter and Beth as one of Marilou's attendants. There was lots of outstanding music, as always. One of Jay's friends from high school was the leader of The Streetnix, an a cappella quartet that did amazing things with their voices. They performed at the wedding ceremony and also at the reception. A makeshift quartet dressed with their suit jackets on backwards entertained us with a special rendition of *Hello, Mary Lou*. This wedding, though beautiful, had a melancholy side for me. With Marilou's marriage, our nest was truly empty. Jay had accepted the position of Youth Pastor at the Trulls Road Free Methodist Church in Courtice, Ontario so they left the day after the wedding to embark on their new career. It was one of the saddest moments of my life. I thought my heart would break as I said my goodbyes.

Marilou and Jay Mowchenko

Chapter 27:

1990—My Parents Return to Saskatchewan

In 1990 we had other changes in our lives that were both good and bad. In the spring of that year it became apparent that my mom and dad could not continue to live in their condominium in New Westminster. The decision was made to sell their condo and come to live with us in Eyebrow. Their stay lasted about a week! By the time Keith was on the bus to B.C. to bring their car and other stuff back, Mom had decided she couldn't live in a little place like Eyebrow, especially since I was gone three days a week to Moose Jaw, leaving her and Dad alone.

So back they went to B.C., briefly moving in with my sister, but, of course, that didn't work either. They rented an apartment in Wesley Manor, a seniors' residence, but Dad's health was declining and Mom couldn't cope. My sister, Eveline, called me to say that they had to come where I was, that she could no longer handle the stress of being responsible for their care.

So to Moose Jaw they came, where we were now living. We found a lovely private home for them, Chez Nous, which was a beautifully decorated old building, full of antiques. It had formerly been a Catholic boys' school. The first room they were in was a large one but it soon became apparent that they couldn't stay there because Dad wandered in the night and Mom, who was a notoriously light sleeper, couldn't get her rest. So they moved to private rooms. Mom was extremely discontented with life as it had turned on her. She couldn't handle Dad's inability to care for her in the way she was used to. He had always been a dedicated husband, at one point as an expression of his love for Mom, even kissing her feet. He had had quadruple heart by-pass surgery in 1988, after which he suffered a stroke that left him in a coma for several days. When I got there to visit following that surgery, I was met by Shirley with the statement, "I hope you brought clothes for a funeral." He did survive but his short-term memory was deeply affected. He was never the same again. Most of his life he had kept a daily diary but after his stroke, he never wrote another page.

Mom had suffered ill-health for years – starting with a broken vertebrae in her back when she was in her 60s, followed by a detached retina which affected her eyesight for the rest of her life, followed by colon cancer surgery from which she never fully recovered. She was insistent that she not have a colostomy since her mother, who had had rectal cancer, had one and she had a dread of them. However, in retrospect, she would have been better off had she had one. She experienced bowel problems until her dying day. Add to the physical problems, the fact was that she had been close to a nervous breakdown for many years, even before she went to Brazil. That experience as missionaries for almost three years only made her condition worse. Learning a new language, coping with the bugs and the unfamiliar surroundings in the interior of Brazil, planting a church in an unwelcoming environment, and dealing with the stresses that my little brother Ross was having, were very difficult. When they sent Ross back to Canada to be cared for by a family in Manitoba, it was heartbreaking for Mom. She was fragile, to say the least.

Chapter 28:

Life With Mother

Sometimes I don't even like to think of those years that I was the sole caregiver for my parents. Dad was always sweet and appreciative of everything anyone did for him. However, we soon found that he needed nursing care so in 1992 we placed him in St. Anthony's Nursing Home, the same one where Marilou worked. He was never a problem. He didn't remember much about his present, like what he had for dinner or what my job was or where I lived, but he could talk about the past and he could still pray with the old fervour whenever he had opportunity. We had a time of singing hymns not long before he died and he sang along, remembering all the words of the songs.

My precious mother, Isabel Campbell in happier times!

Mom, however, was another story. There was always something wrong with the room she was in, or the frequency of my visits, or the meals she was served, or the care she received. After three different rooms we had moved her into, each time hanging her pictures as quickly as possible in order to make it seem more like home, she decided she must have more independence so we found an apartment in which she received her dinner at noon. She lasted there about nine months - which had a positive side because she was there when Dad died and she could have private visits with the family. When we thought she was no longer safe there, because she began to roam around at night, we found a different care home – which she despised. I didn't care for it either because I felt she wasn't treated with respect. To make a bad situation worse, her first roommate had Alzheimer's and brushed her teeth in the toilet! That was the last straw for Mom. In spite of everything Mom had lost, one of them was not her mind! So after that experience, Chez Nous looked pretty good! But there were two different rooms there before she settled in. It was the best and the worst of times. The best because of the visits and phone calls from my family who cared about me as well as our parents. And the worst because of the criticism from my mom which was almost constant.

One day she was particularly angry with me because I refused to look for another place for her. She said she was going to get a taxi and look herself and then she gave me the lowest possible blow when she said, "I know you could take me for all I've got…" She knew I had power of attorney for her affairs so she used it as a weapon to try to control me. Other accusations were very hard to take – like the day I knocked at her door and heard her ask, "Who's there?" When I responded, "It's your daughter," she replied, "I didn't know I had a daughter!"

I have tried to excuse her and say that she didn't know what she was saying and she really didn't mean it but that didn't make it easier to take. It was in those months that I began to feel that I never had pleased her. When she wanted to lash out at me for something I had done or neglected to do, she would bring up something from the past, like the time when I had stolen money from her, something which I had later confessed and even paid restitution for. Another time when I faced her up to the fact that things she said hurt me, she reminded me I had hurt her too when I was two years old. She was referring to the time when I had been sent away from home for about a month when Shirley was born. When I returned I was aloof and that hurt her. Or when I refused to give her enemas (and on the one occasion when I tried and failed) she would remind me that I was no nurse. Both of my sisters were nurses so she had much more confidence in their abilities in that department. Another day when she remarked, "You are not like your sisters," and wouldn't say why, I said, "Do you mean I am not as loving as my sisters?" She admitted that that's how she felt.

Since she has been gone I have tried to remember the good things about Mom and to realize that she had a very hard life. Dad was quite demanding of her. I remember her telling me about one night when she was so exhausted she had retired early. But Dad thought she needed to go to prayer meeting so she dutifully got out of bed, got dressed and went to fulfill his wishes. He would take preaching points and expect her to carry on preaching on the home circuit.

Her childhood was quite painful for her too because her dad died with a ruptured appendix at 37, leaving her mother with seven children under 12. Raised in Kingston, Ontario of wealthy parents, Grandma was unable to cope with life on the homestead in rural Saskatchewan. Mom tells of one day when her mother was off to town, leaving her in charge. Her two-year old sister got into the lye which had been put in the chamber pots under the beds and burnt her mouth badly. They had no phone so Mom's brother went to the neighbour's to call to town where Grandma was shopping. Another time when Mom was only ten because it was before Grandpa died, she was home with the younger children when a fierce snowstorm came up. Her parents were forced to remain overnight in the home they were visiting. Grandpa said, "What about the children?" and Grandma simply replied, "Dotty (Mom's pet name) will look after things."

She worked hard in the fields and was forced to quit school after completing Grade eight in order to help on the farm. Her heart was set on taking a stenographer's course in Winnipeg, where it had been arranged that she would stay with a friend. But her step-father refused to give her the bus fare to go. The family was very unhappy when Grandma married my step-grandfather. Seven inches shorter (Grandma was 5′ 9″) and 13 years younger, he was very jealous of Grandma's children. His attitude made it impossible for my older uncles to work with him so they all moved to northern Saskatchewan where they eked out a living in the bush near Loon Lake. One of my uncles left the area and became a little more prosperous. This second marriage produced a son who continues to farm on the same homestead to this day. The difference in age between my grandparents turned out to a blessing because Grandpa was able to look after Grandma when she had deteriorating health as she got older. She lived to be 94.

In the early years of Grandma's marriage, my grandpa was not a Christian. He was a miserable person who had a particular dislike for my dad (I think because Dad was such a happy person). At the table, he would pass the food in the opposite direction, rather than pass it directly to my dad. When Mom and Dad were married he refused to come down from upstairs in their home. But one summer he gave his heart to the Lord and became a transformed, new person. That's the only way we ever knew him, as a sweet, loving grandpa who gave us lots of hugs.

Chapter 29:

The Passing of a Patriarch

We buried my dad in Moose Jaw in May of 1993. It was a joyful celebration of a life totally dedicated to the Lord. Mom was on a cloud that day as we sang the old hymns and gospel songs that Dad loved. We three girls sang one of his favourites, "Heaven Came Down." Dad knew by personal experience what it was like for heaven to come down and glory fill his soul. Dad always lived his faith.

But after Dad's death, Mom continued to struggle and when we moved to Weyburn she was forced to make another adjustment to a nursing home there where she missed the friends in Moose Jaw who were faithful to visit her. On one occasion when I was very discouraged about Mom's unhappiness with me and with life, I talked to the administrator of the home she was in. I told her that no matter how often I visited Mom it was never enough. She suggested that I not visit her as often. "Leave her for a week and then maybe she'll appreciate you more," she advised. I could hardly believe it when we got a phone call the next day to say that she had fallen and broken her

Dad, Murdo Campbell at Chez Nous with his beloved Bible

hip! We couldn't neglect her in the hospital so between the two of us we visited her there every day.

Marilou was married the same year that Dad died. She worked at St. Anthony's Nursing Home on the men's ward at the time so she felt it keenly when suddenly he was gone. The memories of his home going will forever remain in my mind. After working nights, Marilou came home to say that Grandpa wasn't doing well. Since he had no interest in eating, the administration asked if we would like him to be taken to the hospital and put on IV to prolong his life. Mom and Dad had both given us living wills requesting that we not do that, knowing that when the time came to die, they were ready.

Marilou and I spent the day there, spelled off by Keith. In the evening just Marilou and I were there and we knew the end was drawing near. The Sister who was in charge of palliative care was with us whenever we wanted her to be and she was such a comfort. She got a cassette tape of hymns for Dad to listen to, putting the plugs in his ears because she assured us that hearing is the last sense to go. She lifted up his pant legs and showed us the mottling of his skin which is part of the dying process. She lovingly patted his hand. Although he wasn't conscious, we sang to him. How poignant were the lines in *"My Jesus, I Love Thee." "I will love Thee in life, I will love Thee in death, And praise Thee as long as Thou lendest me breath. And say when the death dew lies cold on my brow, If ever I loved Thee, my Jesus 'tis now."* That was surely the way he would have felt had he been conscious. Sometimes I wish he would have sat up in bed and smiled and saw a vision of Jesus but nothing like that happened. He just slipped away. By eleven o'clock he took his last breath. One comforting memory was the prayer that came over the intercom in that Catholic nursing home, praying for the dying and for the families of the dying. I felt the strength of that prayer.

In spite of all the stress I had been under with the care of Mom, the day before she died in December of 1998 she was bright and happy and we had one of the best visits we had had with her. Quite often Keith and I went at different times but this particular day we had gone together. She had been asked to say grace at the noon meal and we were told that she prayed with a strong voice. We had a good hour with her when she was upbeat and I was glad I had bent over to kiss her good-bye that day (sometimes I was upset with her and refused). At two o'clock the next morning we received a call that she had fallen in the night and was gone. Her funeral service too was a celebration. She was now reunited with Dad in heaven, we were confident of that. All five of us kids gave her a tribute, all seeing her life from a different perspective. She had been a dedicated mother who had sacrificed much so that we could have the things we needed. She had a particular affinity for her sons and they had nothing but wonderful memories. She had also loved all the in-laws. Although there were times when she was unkind to me, she was always nice to Keith. I was happy for that.

I cherish many precious memories of her life. I choose to remember the good things—like her willingness to be a servant, her love for her Lord, and her many gifts that she shared with her family. I am particularly proud of her handiwork, my favourite being a crocheted tablecloth that graces my dining room table. She was always a gracious hostess, serving delicious meals to family and visitors alike.

Chapter 30:

Campbell Family Reunions

Our first Campbell family reunion was held in Dallas, Texas in 1973 where we spent Christmas together at Shirley and Alan Hull's new home. It was a memorable experience. It was a thrill for Dad to have all his children and grandchildren together. Shirley's new home accommodated all 25 of us. Dad took a tour of that house with his tape-recorder in tow, expressing his admiration for everything he saw. We drove to Dallas from Roblin, while all the rest of the family, except my parents, flew. It was a time when there was a shortage of gas and some people advised us rather strongly not to be travelling. But we experienced no problems.

Our family at the Dallas Reunion in 1973

We had a great time making memories. Our children got acquainted with their cousins while we adults got reacquainted with each other because we didn't have a lot of contact during the preceding years. Near the end, Mother, who had been suffering from bad nerves for some years, informed my dad that they must go home. I was somewhat upset because Shirley had arranged a quiet place for them to stay, away from the noise and confusion of her home. Although Dad didn't want to leave, to keep Mom happy, he felt he had no choice. I felt sad for him.

Our second reunion was planned for 1988 in June at Banff, Alberta. The weather was extremely inclement and we found ourselves indoors rather than enjoying times in the beautiful outdoors. Rod had prepared t-shirts for everyone with Mom and Dad's picture on the front but we never got to wear them. Some went horseback riding and golfing in the rain. Dad wasn't able to be there because he had had bypass surgery earlier and still wasn't well enough to attend. One of the benefits for our immediate family was that we spent time together since we were living some distance apart. We did have family times all together and especially enjoyed the worship time on Sunday morning with different ones participating and Cam preaching. Ross's son, Chad said he was the best preacher he ever heard!

The next reunion was in 1993 following Marilou's wedding. By this time, some of the grandchildren were married and Dad was no longer with us. We used the Blue Lounge at Aldersgate College as our base of operations. We had a talent show (which was hilarious with skits that we will never forget!), a sing song, celebrated Rod's birthday, and had a service of worship on Sunday. Eveline's grandchildren entertained us with their musical abilities, Tara playing the piano and the others singing. We ate in the dining room with the college cooks providing excellent meals. We had planned to have a baseball game but the mosquitoes were so ferocious that we had to confine our activities to indoors. The brave souls who went golfing in the morning were almost carried away! One of the highlights of that reunion was Rod's Ferrari which he had shipped up for the occasion. What a head-turning vehicle in our area of Moose Jaw! Keith was on edge the whole time it was parked in our garage, paranoid that some disaster might befall such an expensive car! Elena, who was only three, would ride the tricycle in the driveway and Keith watched like a hawk to see that she didn't get near the Ferrari!

When Rod had his new mansion built in Malibu, California he invited us down for another reunion in 1999. What a wonderful setting! Overlooking the beautiful Pacific Ocean, a swimming pool on site, spacious rooms inside where we all could meet (49 of us, as I recall), it was an ideal place. With some of the participants at the reunion having new babies, the entertainment wasn't quite as spectacular as the previous one, but we still had our team cheers and activities. Eveline, Shirley and I sang a trio, one of the McGuire Sisters songs, a memory of days gone by. A par-three golf course provided a place to show our talents (or lack thereof). In the worship time we enjoyed singing together, thankful for Rod's beautiful grand piano accompaniment. The speaker of the day was Scott Hull, Shirley's son, a very bright personable young man.

The last siblings get-together at a mini-reunion in B.C.

We were grateful for the most recent reunion held in 2011 in Canmore, Alberta. Most of the family stayed in a hotel in the city while the siblings met in a rustic, log building outside of town. The scenery was gorgeous. A helicopter ride (thanks to Rod's generosity) gave us a breathtaking view of the area while some went water-rafting, another memorable experience. We enjoyed great food, celebrated our Scottish roots with a bagpiper (Sandra's great-nephew), had fun times doing our usual "Wacky Olympics" and a Sunday morning church service in which Jay preached and talked about some of Mom and Dad's legacy. Marilou had made a CD from Mom and Dad's old record and played it for us, nostalgic for some of us for sure. The missing member this time was Eveline, though Jim attended. She had died in May of 2010, quite unexpectedly although she had been in poor health for some time. Jim who was showing signs of dementia, had been her caregiver and could hardly cope with her loss. He was later placed in a home and passed away in February of 2014, interestingly enough, on my birthday.

Chapter 31:

More Changes, Some Sad, Some Happy

Another big change came in our lives when Aldersgate College closed in 1995. Keith was left without a job in April of that year. He had turned 64 in February but we had hoped to work a few more years beyond 65, at least part time, so that we could travel, not only to see the world but also to visit our children and grandchildren. However, the Scotts, one of our best couple friends, who were building a cabin at Arlington Beach, offered Keith a job for the summer so he commuted there for several weeks. My job in the office as the president's secretary was terminated so I was on Unemployment Insurance for several months. I loved working and missed the college community in which we had lived. Our house was right on campus. While the students were there, we enjoyed watching them out our front windows as they went back and forth from the administration/classroom building to their dorm. It was fun to watch friendships develop into romances. Keith valued the relationships he built with the students. Although we had made some good friends at the Moose Jaw church, we felt the loss of the college faculty and staff as they began to move away. After much distress, we sold our lovely home and moved to Weyburn.

It was interesting that our choice for retirement was Weyburn. It was largely because the church was thriving and the people were upbeat. We wanted to be around positive people. I applied for the part-time secretary job at the church and worked there for five years until we left the West. It felt like pay-back time for all the years that I had typed the weekly bulletin with no remuneration. It was exciting to be part of such a growing, vital body of believers. I led the senior Bible study and formed many lasting friendships.

Our new life in Weyburn began in a rented apartment just half a block from the site where Keith managed the building of our second new home, this one more beautiful than the first. After its completion when people asked me if there was anything I would have changed about it, my answer has always been No. It was perfect! It had a large cathedral-style window in the living room, a French pocket door from the kitchen to dining area, another pocket door into the little computer room off the kitchen, a laundry area on the main floor, an en suite complete bathroom in our bedroom, a walk-in closet, a heated double garage with an entrance to the house, a big hall and living room which was large enough to hold the piano, and a full basement which Keith had finished beautifully. He had one of the best gardens he'd ever had in our spacious backyard. All the five years we were there, there were no houses on either side of us. Keith liked that because he could park his old Toyota truck beside the house. Surprisingly, by the time we left the area in 2001, houses were being built on both sides.

Our beautiful new home in Weyburn

Although we never lived close to Marilou in the years after her marriage, we endeavoured to visit as often as possible. In 1997 Jay and Marilou moved to Abbotsford, BC so that Jay could partner with Cam in the Mountain Ridge Church. Two precious gifts from that period of time were the children who were both born there - Keisha Grace on December 20, 1997 and Joshua Taylor on November 23, 1999. It was difficult being so far away when our "baby" was experiencing labour, neither one of which was an easy delivery. We got the call from Jay at 8 a.m. on December 19th that Marilou was in labour but we went to bed that night hearing nothing more. Keisha finally arrived by Caesarean section about 6 a.m. on December 20th after hours of labour. I'm sure it was the longest night of my life. When Joshie came, the labour was not as long and fortunately, he was born naturally, though there was some stress because the cord was wrapped around his neck. Just a month after Joshie's birth, Jay and Marilou were on their way back to Ontario - now farther than ever from us. It was an intensely lonely feeling. While they were in B.C. we were able to get in the car and in 24 hours be with them. Such has been the story of our lives!

Jay & Marilou with their children, Keisha and Joshua

Chapter 32:

The Realities of Life in Pastoral Ministry

We basically had very little money during most of our pastoral ministry years so we learned to live frugally. To be truthful, we lived below the poverty line. But we didn't really feel poor. Once when Keith asked Beth is she thought we were poor, she said no, that we were rich. But the fact is that our income was higher during our tenure at the college in Moose Jaw and in our retirement years at Weyburn than it ever had been before. In our first church we had no salary and only received what the people "felt led" to give us. Some people only gave when the pastor called on them - one way to get him to visit! We got some of that in produce, as had my parents in the early years. Our first salary was in Broadview where we received $1800 per year. It only bought necessities. It was not much better in Brandon and even in Weyburn where our congregation was much bigger, we were not overpaid. One of our parishioners jokingly remarked on one occasion, "If the Lord will keep you humble, we'll keep you poor." And basically they were true to their word!

We were able to accumulate some of the extras because I always worked part-time, much of it as a substitute teacher. Later I did office work which I found less stressful than teaching. And Keith, ever the jack-of-all-trades, always had jobs on the side. We always bought new cars and even saved for retirement. That enabled us to buy our new home in Moose Jaw. We also had some help with that when my parents gave us an early inheritance after selling their condominium. We believe strongly in the principle of tithing and felt that God blessed us for our faithfulness. He promised to supply our needs and He always has - sometimes through others and sometimes through hard work. We are deeply grateful to my brother Rod, who has been blessed with the ability to make money. His generosity has lightened our load on many occasions. During those difficult years of caring for Mom, Rod surprised us with the gift of two leased Ford cars. The first was a Mystique, a car I loved to drive, then a Windstar van which helped us in our move to Ontario as it was able to carry breakable things that wouldn't fit in the moving van. Keith always said he would never drive a Ford unless someone gave him one. So that was the one and would only time for that! One of the gifts Rod had given us for our new home in Moose Jaw was a light fixture for above our dining room table but we felt we had to leave it behind when we left Weyburn. To my surprise, our house in Courtice had an identical fixture in the dining room!

Our children were ambitious and were able to work to pay for their own education. Unfortunately, we were never able to give them a lot. Sometimes we assisted them by giving them free room and board while they worked in the summer, or loaning them money to buy their first car, which we did for Beth. We are grateful that they never seemed to resent having to pay their own way. Our children have always been a source of joy. They were great examples in our churches and shared in the work we were doing. Their contributions were many, particularly in the music department. During the time in the 70s when we were experiencing revival, we had a little game that we played. There was a lot of emphasis on Christ being on the throne of our lives and not us, so that when someone was acting in an un-Christlike manner, we would ask the question, "Who's on the throne?" It always worked. When the children had grown up and left to establish their own homes, we felt a great vacancy.

Chapter 33:

Memorable Travelling Experiences

When the children were home we were able to enjoy several trips, most of them to B.C. where Mom and Dad, my sister Eveline and her family as well as Keith's brother, Glenn and his family lived. One year when Beth and Cam were young we took the trip with Keith's mom and dad, that time stopping in Yellowstone Park and having our first glimpse of Old Faithful. When Marilou was a teenager, we visited the Black Hills where Mount Rushmore and the Passion Play left a lasting impression.

In 1980 our family all journeyed to B.C. to help Mom and Dad celebrate their 50th wedding anniversary. It was a fun event when we reenacted some of their life experiences. The only disappointing thing about it was that Rod was in England and couldn't be there.

On one of our many trips West when the children were young we had a mishap in Kelowna, B.C. where our car was rear-ended. It was on our way home and when we travelled we rarely made any unnecessary stops along the way. We had to report the accident which held us up for some time. The good part was that the trunk would still close so no great harm was done. However, Keith was not happy with the delay. As we got going, he was complaining a little about the accident when our wise young son came up with an appropriate response. "Dad," he said, "There is nothing we can do about it so let's just forget it!" He had a wonderful way of looking at the positive side of everything, something that has served him well through life.

It has been in our later years that we have also been able to take some wonderful trips to places in the world we have always wanted to see. Our first trip was to the Holy Land. Our conference superintendent, Jack Walrath, made it possible for pastors to have this unforgettable experience at an affordable price. It was wonderful to "walk where Jesus walked." A highlight for me was singing "The Stranger of Galilee" while riding across the Sea of Galilee in a boat, the very sea that was so familiar to Jesus and his disciples. We saw the valley where David slew Goliath and marveled at the diminutive size of the country of Israel where so much biblical history has taken place. Visiting the cave in Bethlehem where Jesus was born and viewing the tomb at Gordon's Calvary where we had communion in the garden were memorable.

Another trip that we took with Keith's sister Evelyn and her husband Allan Green, which was partly a working experience, was to Haiti where we stayed with missionaries and helped with projects around the mission. The guys built a corner cupboard, we reupholstered a couch and chair, and did other odd jobs that the missionaries couldn't find time to do. We spent time with Warren and Della Land, outstanding missionaries whom we had admired since they had been guests at our summer church camp. The experiences affected all of our senses - the smells of the market in downtown Port au Prince - the sights of the innumerable beggars sitting on the streets and the adorable kindergarten children who sang so lustily for us - the taste of freshly baked mango pie - the feeling of awe at the fervour of the Haitian Christians who made worship such a great celebration. It was quite overwhelming. When we got back to Florida where we encountered overweight, complaining people who had so much, we could hardly bring ourselves to even go shopping. We had never seen a poverty-stricken country like Haiti, and within such a short distance of the U.S. coast. We will never forget the joy that the Christians expressed. Keith preached through an interpreter, a wonderful experience for him.

To celebrate our 40th wedding anniversary in 1995 we took a tour to England, Wales and Scotland. That was a highlight - so much history there! We had a fabulous tour guide who furnished us with loads of fascinating information. She was an expert on the Royal Family and we heard all the family secrets, past and present. I never tired of the awe-inspiring cathedrals, castles and places that we've studied in history but never had the opportunity to see. Our hotel in London was within walking distance of Buckingham Palace and Westminster Abbey. The first night on our walk we came across a sign outside of the Abbey which announced an organ recital which was taking place just as we were there. It was a little late but I knew I'd never have an opportunity to be there again so said I was going. Keith didn't want to spend the money but another member of our tour was interested so the two of us went in. When we entered they told us that we would only have to pay half the price of admission since the concert was partly over. We sat in the choir loft a very short distance from the organist - it was wonderful!

At Buckingham Palace in London in 1995

In addition to our initial trip with Dave and Norma Scott that went back to Expo in 1967, we continued our friendship over the years, enjoying several more travelling experiences with them. They proved to be wonderful travelling companions. We were part of a tour group that went to China in October, 1999, with retired missionary, Lavern Snider as the host. We visited Beijing, Shanghai and Hong Kong. That brought us face-to-face with centuries of history. To walk the Great Wall of China was unforgettable. It's hard to visualize the expansiveness of it from pictures. To stand in Tienamin Square reminded us of the sad events that took place there a few years before. We were taken to places where we received communist propaganda, where you wondered how much of what they were saying was actually true. We visited a kindergarten with happy, well-fed children. Never in our lives have we ever seen so many bicycles (9 million in Beijing)!

Our memorable trip to Shanghai, China with best friends, Dave & Norma Scott

Sometimes it looked downright dangerous to see them weaving through the heavy traffic in the cities. We stayed in the most beautiful hotels we had seen anywhere - all new and opulently furnished. By the time we got out of Beijing and Shanghai where we were fed the same strange kinds of food (not much like our Chinese food), we were so ready for some Western fare. Pizza Hut was truly a welcome sight! We were happy to meet Hong Kong missionaries, Jim and Margaret Nelson, who spent some time with us, and Loren and Sylvia Van Tassel (she was Canadian) who were teaching in mainland China and had come to Hong Kong to meet our group. We attended a worship service with Chinese Christians in Hong Kong and enjoyed a meal with some of them after. It was the fulfillment of a dream for us to go to Hong Kong since we had applied to serve there as missionaries back in the 50's. When you hear the difficult Chinese languages spoken, you realize how impossible it would have been to become proficient in them - but we did at least get to see the beautiful colony!

Another travel experience was the year that Rod invited us to visit them in France where they rented a villa above the French Riviera, near Cannes. Distinctive about that visit were the fresh baguettes we had every morning for breakfast, the nude beaches, the visit to Monaco where we saw the world-famous casino and race track through the downtown area. At the conclusion of our visit Rod arranged a hotel in downtown Paris which was near to the Arch de Triumph so we had the amazing experience of roaming through the area in the evening, taking in all the sights, including the brightly lit Eiffel Tower. On the taxi drive from the airport we declared we had never seen gridlock like we saw it there! The light turned from green to red several times and still no one moved. Finally our driver managed to wiggle around some of the traffic to take another route.

In 2002, we visited the Maritimes with our good friends, Dave and Norma, staying in five Bed & Breakfasts in New Brunswich, Nova Scotia and Prince Edward Island. It was a wonderful experience - enjoying lots of seafood, including lobster, seeing the red soil of PEI, the Fortress of Louisbourg, the Alexander Graham Bell National Historic Site, the Halifax Citadel, Green Gables, Peggy's Cove, whale watching on the Bay of Fundy, and attending a Ceildhi. This was to be our last trip with the Scotts. Dave, who suffered with pancreatic cancer for several years, died in 2004. We visited Norma in Florida one winter after Dave died. One of the most positive people I have known, she was afflicted with breast cancer, then colon cancer and finally bladder cancer. When she died in 2009, I felt that I had lost a truly great friend.

To celebrate our 50th anniversary in 2005 we went on our first cruise. We boarded the ship in Los Angeles, then saw many interesting sites as we stopped at several ports in Mexico, including Cabo San Lucas, and Acapulco. At Huatulco we simply shopped. A bus trip in Puntarenas, Costa Rica, afforded us the opportunity to see many crocodiles lazing in the sun. The most significant and memorable experience was going through the Panama Canal. Our journey continued to the Caribbean where we visited Aruba and Jamaica, then to Fort Lauderdale, Florida from where we flew home. The whole experience was incredible - the amount of delicious food, the menu choices, the decorative food items, the ice sculptures, the wonderful entertainment, the fun games, the fantastic accommodations, the service provided, all enjoyed with a couple from our church. It was like living in the lap of luxury for 15 days!

During our first few years living in Ontario we went on two bus trips—one to Branson, Missouri and another to Lancaster, Pennsylvania. They were both great experiences with good friends. In 2012 we had our second (and probably last) cruise which was seven days in the Caribbean. It was a fun trip with two couples from our church who proved to be wonderful travelling companions. We visited St. Maarten, St. Lucia, Grenada, Bonaire and Aruba. The reality is that my partner now is a very reluctant traveler so our trips are few and not very far. We do enjoy time in the summer at our trailer at Wesley Acres Camp, about two hours away. It's a beautiful spot and we spend time attending the two family camps in the summer, 50+ retreat in the fall and other times when we visit with friends who spend the summer there.

Chapter 34:

My Taylor Family Connections

Being part of the Taylor family has been a blessing from God. They lived much closer than my parents or siblings and their place became "home" to me. From 1959 to 1968 we had lived only 100 miles away from them. So when the children were small we would go there for a break fairly often. We always received a warm welcome, particularly from Keith`s dad. I loved that man! Whenever I would sing he would have tears in his eyes. When I sat on the couch he would sit down beside me and put his arm around me. I really felt loved by him. That`s why I was so sad when he died very suddenly one night in June of 1969, at the age of 73. Ever since, I have had a dread of phone calls at 2 a.m.

I think Mother Taylor loved me but she didn`t show it like Dad. I`m not sure she approved of everything I did and sometimes I wondered if she thought her son had married the right woman! She was a very industrious person. When we visited the farm where they lived, I would be almost embarrassed when I got up, to see her countertops lined with pies and cakes. She also had the dinner (that's what it was, not lunch) well on the way which, by the way, was always served at 12 o'clock sharp! She was a plain cook, but a good one. We had great

Jack & MyrtleTaylor, known to me as Mother & Dad Taylor

conversations and I loved to hear of her early experiences as a teacher in isolated locations. We had lots of good games of Scrabble together, a passion we shared. She was a master of the art of quilt-making . All of her children and grandchildren treasure her gifts, passed down through the generations.

My mother-in-law and I had some differences of opinion, especially in regards to potty training. She believed that you should start early, putting them in training panties well before the age of two. She claimed that Evelyn was trained at the age of eight months. Our children did not train early and I was terribly frustrated when I followed her advice. I decided to follow Dr. Spock's advice instead and not even start training until the children were two. Even then it was not a quick process.

My in-laws were wonderful babysitters and we would know that the children were in excellent hands when we went away. We heard later that some of the family thought we had abused the privileges but Mom and Dad never gave us that impression. The only thing that used to irritate me was when we returned and the children would be whiny, she would say, "We never saw any of that." They were always on their best behavior with Grandma and Grandpa Taylor.

Some of the Taylors have become not only family but close friends over the years. I helped plan family reunions and even wrote a little booklet on Mother Taylor`s life. I sat many hours with her taking notes. She had a very interesting life. She was indeed a wise woman who raised seven children, all active in the church and serving the Lord.

Keith's mother died the same year as dad, in February of 1993, just days before her 94th birthday. She was buried on my birthday. The celebration of her life was a blessing to the family. She had lived a good life, being able to live in her own little apartment until a few months before her death, when she had gone into a nursing home. She was happy there and often talked about the kindness of her caregivers. She would sit at the front window and enjoy watching people coming and going. Her mind remained intact, with the exception of a few memory lapses. Her body sometimes let her down, mostly her arthritic knees.

One of the poignant memories of that time when we were preparing for the burial of Keith's mom was when we went to pick out the casket with his brother, Don. He had been Keith's partner in farming but was now suffering from early dementia. Consequently, he wasn't able to help with many of the decisions. The reason we were involved in the planning was because Evelyn, the family member living closest to her mom, was in Ontario with her daughter, Patricia who just had a baby boy the day before Mother died. We felt a sense of loss in the death of such a strong maternal figure who had been such a great, positive influence on her family and on others she had known.

The Taylor siblings: Roy & Helen Caswell, Don & Lyla Taylor, Glenn & Dolores Taylor, Keith & Joan Taylor, Evelyn & Allan Green, Betty & Martin Taylor, Joyce & Derrell Rodine

One of the sad things when we made the decision to leave the prairies was leaving Keith's family behind. They have become very dear to me since I became one of them. In fact, in some ways they were closer than my own sisters, simply because I have spent so much more time with them. That is especially true of Evelyn and it is also because Keith has been a life-time friend with her husband Allan. But until Allan's death we were able to see them at least once a year, sometimes more because when they have visited their daughters in Ontario they have been to our place. It is difficult to see family members having health problems and then dying – but that is life when you get to our age. But then we really don't want the alternative to growing old!

Chapter 35:

Opportunities to Develop My Leadership Skills

That God had gifted me with some leadership qualities was evident pretty young. I always liked to be in charge, whether it was playing school or playing with friends. It is probably the reason why my favourite sister was Shirley because she was more compliant by nature than my older sister so I got to lead as a young child.

This innate ability led me to take on leadership roles wherever we went. It gave me opportunities to be part of the community as I was eventually president of some of the organizations I belonged to - like Music Festival committees and Music Parents Association. As a teenager in the church, I was leader of the young people's group. Later I was director of the Christian Youth Crusaders and president of the Women's Ministries. Before we even got to Brandon, one of the ladies had announced that I was to be the president of the Women's Missionary Society, which it was called at that time. There didn't seem to be any consideration to the fact that I was only 25 and had never even been to a WMS meeting in my life!

One of my most encouraging requests to be a leader came from the Weyburn young people who were in my Bible quizzing group. One of them met me at our camp and said they would like me to be the Youth Advisor at the Conference level. It was a privilege to work with the youth and be part of their rallies and camps that I attended. I was also elected to the position of president of the Women's Ministries International and served there for several years. That afforded me the opportunity to attend the General Conference at our church world headquarters at Indianapolis, Indiana (formerly Winona Lake), a great experience. I served as a member of the Ministerial Education and Guidance Committee for many years, first in the Canada West Conference and later as part of the Canada East region. That was an amazing challenge, as we met and interviewed potential ministerial candidates. A highlight for me was being elected as a "member at large" of the Board of Administration in Western Canada, the first woman to serve in that position. The church has been a big part of my life and it has been great to be part of the inner workings of the church.

My most recent leadership roles have been in the Trulls Road Free Methodist Church which we have attended since moving to Ontario. For five-and-one-half years I served on the Official Board, most of that time as Chair. I have also served for several years on the committee that plans social events for the 50+ age group. I was privileged to be part of the Search Committee when we were looking for a pastor. I have felt that God directed us to the man, Brian Bell, who has been our pastor for the past five years.

Chapter 36:

Our Final Move - to Ontario

Over several years Beth had been suggesting to us that we should move to Ontario. But Keith was quite adamant that he would never do that so it was always put on the back burner. However, when Marilou and Jay were settled in Ontario and no family member was closer than Abbotsford, BC, we began to think that perhaps it wasn't such a bad idea. Keith had been working hard all the time we lived in Weyburn, mostly painting, as well as managing the building of a new home for a friend. So he was accumulating enough money to make the move possible. It was a major accomplishment.

In preparation for our move, we had an auction sale, packed up what we needed to take, hired a moving van and on August 31, 2001 we left Weyburn behind. The people gave us a great send-off. Derrell and Joyce hosted a family gathering at their place with 35 in attendance. Then the church had a potluck supper with about 100 in attendance. There were songs, and tributes from those we had come to love - I remarked in my diary at the end of that day that it was like attending your own funeral! We drove away with good feelings - that we had made a contribution to people's lives. Keith had a very strong bond with his coffee buddies. It even included the mayor because he was one of the people for whom Keith had painted, since he owned several properties around the city. I had served as secretary at the church most of the time we lived there. I was still finishing up my work the day we left!

The summer that we moved, the whole family came home for one last get-together on the Prairies. When we sold our house we discovered that the buyers wanted a much earlier closing date than was convenient for us. Because it meant a $5,000 bonus, we had no choice but to find other accommodations. Cam and Vicky stayed with us in the two-bedroom apartment we had moved into. We scrounged around for sleeping quarters for the rest of the family. In my little kitchen I cooked the meals, including a turkey dinner which we ate, picnic-style out on the patio. We made some memories during that time, one being a trip to Cannington Manor, the area where Mother Taylor had grown up and attended school, now a historical landmark with costumed attendants reenacting community life of the past.

One of the challenges we faced with a move to Ontario was buying a house. We lived too far away to contact realtors and look at properties for sale. So we had to depend on Beth to do the house-hunting for us. She found a bungalow in the same area of Courtice where they live. She sent pictures on line so we viewed it all from a distance. She knew what we wanted, particularly for me that I needed a big kitchen with lots of counter space. I always loved baking. Few things makes me feel prouder than to see my counter covered with fresh baked buns and pies. My baking is always a welcome part of family dinners.

Our comfortable home in Courtice

Beth accomplished her task and we have been pleased with her choice. We moved into the house on September 4, 2001, only one week before the tragic events of September 11th. It was hard to leave our beautiful home in Weyburn and certainly we miss some of the luxuries we had there. But we have been happy here with everything that we need. Having passed the 15-year mark, I have concluded that I have lived in this house and community longer than any other. Keith takes great pride in his backyard where he grows tomatoes and raspberries. The front yard has provided the neighbours a viewing of beautiful flowers every summer. Admittedly, my only contribution to all this has been selecting the flowers, coordinating the colours.

The family all together to celebrate our 50th wedding anniversary In 2005

One of the happy events in our lives took place in 2005 when we celebrated our 50th wedding anniversary. Our family planned a wonderful evening for us, complete with dinner and a fabulous program which included family and friends. We will never forget the skit our two sons-in-law presented showing us as they sometimes have seen us! It was hilarious! Except for Eveline, my siblings were there as well as Keith's youngest two siblings and their spouses. Prior to the celebration our family spent a few days together at Ross and Sylvia's cottage. The only thing that put a dampener on the day was the weather. It reminded me of the old song Mrs. Willows, a dear old saint, used to sing, "My didn't it rain!"

My siblings-Ross & Sylvia, Alan & Shirley Hull, Rod & Sandra

We have been blessed with some very special friends in the Trulls Road Free Methodist Church which we attend. I cannot say that I didn`t have some fears when we were moving from the places we had lived all our lives and the family and friends we have shared so many experiences with. But we decided before we came that we were going to like it. Moving across the country is costly business and we knew that it was for keeps. Of course, we knew there was a church family that we would be part of, some of whom we had already met when we visited Beth's family. However, we never dreamed that we could feel so close to people that we've only known for such a short time. We thought that perhaps friendships would be so well established in a community where people had lived their whole lives that we would not be able to break into them. But we have some of the deepest friendships we've ever had. Maybe it's easier when you are not the pastor! By this time, I felt like I was truly out of the fishbowl! Of course, Keith is still called "Pastor" so I will likely always be viewed as the "Pastor's wife."

We are in a weekly Bible study (which I lead) with some of our good friends. Keith has his coffee buddies that are very important to him. I am in a Red Hat group that is purely for fun - eating out once a month dressed up in our purple clothes and red hats. Barry's mom started it with some of her friends and our numbers have dwindled as she and others have passed away. Another pleasure of mine is serving as a volunteer cashier in a Bibles for Missions thrift store for four hours each week. Oh yes, and there's Scrabble! I've already mentioned my involvements there and my passion for the game which never diminishes. Reading is something that I have developed a greater love for. I have been accomplishing my goal to read a book a week. Reading opens up such a wonderful world of experiences.

Playing Scrabble with grandson Justin

Life in Courtice has been rewarding in many ways. The closer bond with the family has been wonderful. We have been able to get to know our grandchildren and be involved in their lives. I was able to use my gift of teaching to assist Shannon, our oldest granddaughter, with her high school and college work. I took refresher courses in Psychology and Sociology as she pursued a two-year course in Early Childhood Education and I worked with her preparing term papers and studying for exams. Her graduation was a highlight for me as well as her. On May 5/05 she wrote me a note which I highly treasure. In it she said, *"I wanted to first of all wish you a happy Mother's Day! What a great mother you are, because you are certainly a great Grandma! I also want to thank you for all the time and effort you've put into my education these last two years. You were so much fun to work with and I enjoyed our times together. I know there were times when it was a lot of hard work and intense studying but we would have fun anyway. I look forward to graduation in June! I'm sure you will be there, cheering right in the front row "partner."*

Our eldest granddaughter Shannon earned her ECE certification in 2005

Another significant experience for us has been the input we have had into the lives of Marilou's children. Every Tuesday Marilou brought Keisha and Joshie to our house for us to babysit while she taught piano through the supper hour. We played together in our basement - the favourite game being dress-up where we reenacted the story of the Three Bears. Keisha was always Goldilocks, Joshie was her little brother and I was Mama Bear. Papa and Baby Bear were stuffed animals. Sometimes on beautiful days we walked to the pond where we fed the ducks and collected trash on the way home. Or we visited the playground in the area. We fed them supper - they loved what I cooked, especially mashed potatoes and gravy, then we took them home and put them to bed. Those were such precious bonding times.

It all came to an end in 2006 when Jay accepted a call to become the senior pastor at the Weyburn Free Methodist Church. It seemed ironic that he was going back to serve the church that we had left in 2001. They had started the Freeway church plant, taking it from a Sunday evening service at the Trulls Road church to a school that they were meeting in on Sunday morning. It was never a booming success which may have caused some of the "faithful" to get discouraged. As a result several families decided to leave which was difficult for Jay and the others who were left. He began to wonder if Freeway was where he should be. We attended their final baptism service where Keisha was baptized and others who had been helped spiritually. There are people who are part of God's Kingdom because of the Freeway. Thankfully, Freeway has continued and is now a growing community.

Chapter 37:

Family Losses

2010 was a year of change with the loss of my sister, Eveline on May 8 and our brother-in-law, Allan Green three days later. We attended both memorial services and were blessed to be part of our family on those occasions. We will always cherish special memories of our loved ones. Since Keith celebrated his 80th birthday in February of 2011, he is very cognizant of the fact that his most productive years are behind him. But we're both thankful that we've been blessed with excellent health and we have had each other for over 60 years.

The first family member in Keith`s family to leave us was Helen`s husband, Roy, from cancer, in 1995. At only 73 he wasn't prepared to die and wouldn't discuss the subject. The last time our kids saw him lying in his bed on morphine, his body full of cancer, he assured them that he would see them "next year." Keith`s brother Don had suffered with dementia and died at the age of 71 in 1997. Lyla, crippled with arthritis and living in a nursing home, followed him in 2000. She was one of the most godly women I have ever known. A victim of rheumatoid arthritis in her 20s, she never complained. Keith`s older brother, Glenn died in 2009, his sister Helen in 2013 at the age of 90. We have good memories of her as we were present to help her celebrate her 90th birthday in August.

2011 brought another significant life-altering event to our family. It represented losses of another kind for Cam and Vicky. It happened on April 23rd, the night before Easter when at 10:30 p.m. we received a heart-stopping phone call from a social worker at the Royal Columbia Hospital in New Westminster, B.C. The message stated that our son and his wife had been involved in a motorcycle accident and he was in critical condition. In my mind, that meant that he might die and I was deeply disturbed. I immediately called Beth (the calm one who keeps her head in all situations) and she made the necessary phone calls to Marilou and then to the Parkins (Vicky's mom and dad) to see what we could find out. In great anxiety we awaited more news. When word came at about 12:30 a.m. that he had stabilized, I was able to put Cam into God's hands and go to sleep. He came very close to losing his life. Actually it was a speedy air ambulance trip to a trauma hospital and a subsequent blood transfusion that saved him.

On Easter Sunday morning our choir presented a musical/drama celebrating the Easter story, with Beth as the director. When we sang with deep conviction and joy the message of Easter that "Jesus is Alive!" Beth and I were also celebrating that Cam was alive! We had never experienced anything like it. That Easter will long live in our memories.

It has been a long, slow, painful recovery for Cam and Vicky. After five years, Cam is now resuming a normal life. Early on, there were recurring bouts of infection which required additional surgeries. Finally in May, 2012, more than a year after his accident, he had a bone transporter put in that would build bone in the five-inch space where the femur bone had been destroyed. In the meantime, for many months he could put no weight on his right leg so he depended on crutches, walker and wheelchair for his mobility. His losses include his ability to work, his motorcycle and the fun times they have experienced over the 20 years he rode safely, and his independence as he had to depend on so many people for support. He has had a total of ten surgeries, the most recent ones to

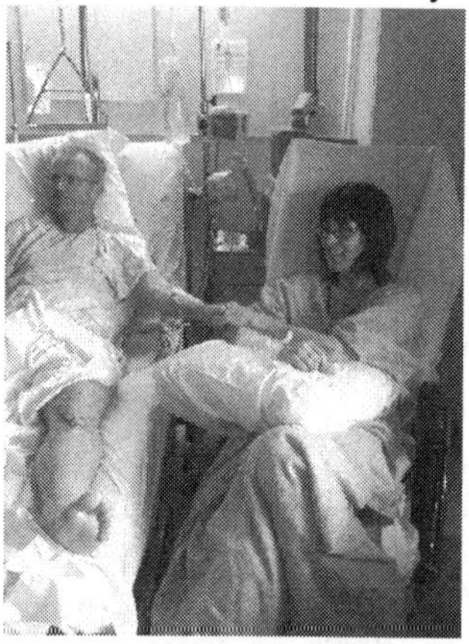

Cam & Vicky recovering in hospital after their near-fatal motorcycle accident

repair his knee, then to take the hardware out of his shoulder. All because a man failed to stop at a stop sign and made a left turn onto the highway right in the motorcycle's path. Sadly, there was nowhere to go.

We have learned many lessons through this experience. First and foremost, we learned how much our family means to us. And we learned how much it hurts to see your children suffering. We have become closer as a family as we rallied around to assist Cam at different times. Marilou, who went out the same time we did shortly after the accident, was able to transport us to and from the hospital. Mother's Day that year provided me an opportunity to be with my son when he was most vulnerable. At that time, he couldn't move without assistance. Beth has made several trips out to be there for moral and physical support. She did a great job of organizing their house since Vicky has suffered as well and her recovery is also slow. Vicky's previous brain tumour surgery had already left her with balance problems and the lack of fine motor skills in her right hand. So she has many struggles with mobility and probably will never completely recover. I went back in September of 2011 and again in May 2012 to be with Cam when he returned home after another surgery, since Vicky had returned to work. That was a blessing as I was able to help with some of the cooking and be there for moral support. I greatly appreciate the time we spent together and all the great talks we had. He's an amazing son! Vicky, too has been amazing in the way she has persevered through so much suffering. She had a recurrence of her brain tumour so they travelled to Japan to have a world-famous surgeon operate in April of 2014. He is quite confident that it will not return.

Chapter 38:

Highlight of 2014 – The Marriage of Our First Grandchild

Though we have experienced loss in our family, we have also gained--a beautiful new granddaughter in the person of Christina Adams. Justin, Beth's youngest, met Christina in 2013 and it was truly a meeting of two soul mates. They were engaged in October after their first date in July and then married in August of 2014. Everything was perfect about the day – the weather, the setting, the

Our family celebrating the marriage of Justin and Christina (Adams) Rawn in 2014

friends and family, the speeches, the food, and above all, the deliriously happy couple. Jay officiated at a meaningful outdoor ceremony which included the washing of each other's feet, a symbol of servanthood. Keisha was part of the music, Shannon and Ryan were attendants and we felt proud to be the grandparents, a distinct honour. Everyone in our family was present except for Caleb who is now living in Yellowknife, NWT – a little out of reach.

The wedding weekend included a mini-reunion with my siblings who came from far away places to be present. After the wedding we enjoyed a ride on the Kingston trolley to visit the historic city where our grandma was originally from and our mother was born. It is a beautiful old place. We felt blessed also to have our immediate family all here for a few days after the wedding to reminisce, eat and play together. We are confident that this newly married couple will be headed toward a long, happy life together. One reason we say this is because they have built their marriage on a solid foundation, Christ being the Center.

Chapter 39:

Our Legacy

2015 made me an octogenarian! My 80th birthday was a memorable event with Marilou and Keisha here to help me celebrate, along with the Rawn family. It was great to also have special friends who live in the area as part of the event. Many lovely things were said that I will forever cherish. 2015 has truly been a year of celebration as our 60th wedding anniversary took place in April. We had a come-and-go afternoon at our home in Courtice in May with 70 in attendance. In June we flew to Saskatchewan where we had another celebration in Marilou and Jay's backyard with 90 attending. It was wonderful to welcome members of our former congregations

The family who were here to help celebrate my 80th birthday in 2015

Our 60th wedding anniversary party at our home in Courtice

Our anniversary celebration at Marilou's in Weyburn

who came to honour us, as well as friends, and relatives from both sides of the family. We have been blessed to have reached this age with our minds and bodies in pretty good condition!

We both desire to leave behind a legacy of faith in a God who never changes, even when everything around us is changing. We deeply value our Christian heritage passed down from both sides of the family and desire that all of our grandchildren will embrace the faith that has been such a vital part of our lives.

Our wonderful children worked together to make our 60th a memorable, happy event

Our children are a source of great joy and pride in that they have followed the Lord and have lived out their lives serving Him and others. There is nothing in this world that is more satisfying than that. We haven't had a lot of this world's goods to give our children but what we have given them is of far greater value than money. We do not feel that our children have suffered by being raised "in a fishbowl." Certainly they were watched but they were constantly affirmed by members of our congregations. I never told them that they were to be examples, but they followed the instruction given in I Timothy 4:12: "Don't let anyone look down on you because you are young, but set an example for the believers in speech, in life, in love, in faith and in purity." That was their way of life. We do not take pride in our success as parents because we have not been perfect by any means. It is only by grace that we can say, To God be the glory!

I end my story with the words of one of my favourite gospel songs, written by Andrae Crouch.

TO GOD BE THE GLORY

How can I say thanks for the things you have done for me?
Things so undeserved, yet you give to prove your love for me.
The voices of a million angels could not express my gratitude;
All that I am and ever hope to be, I owe it all to Thee.

Chorus

To God be the glory, to God be the glory, to God be the glory
For the things he has done.
With his blood he has saved me, with his power he has raised me.
To God be the glory for the things he has done.

Just let me live my life, let it be pleasing Lord to Thee;
And should I gain any praise, let it go to Calvary.
With his blood he has saved me, with his power he has raised me.
To God be the glory for the things he has done.

57772922R00113

Made in the USA
Charleston, SC
25 June 2016